INSTANT
FAVOURITES

Mia Bachmaier & Mike McColl

INSTANT
FAVOURITES

Over 125 easy recipes
FOR YOUR ELECTRIC PRESSURE COOKER

Collins

HarperCollins books may be purchased for educational, business, or sales promotional use through our Special Markets Department.

HarperCollins Publishers Ltd
2 Bloor Street East, 20th Floor
Toronto, Ontario, Canada
M4W 1A8

www.harpercollins.ca

Library and Archives Canada Cataloguing in Publication information is available upon request.

ISBN 978-1-44345-492-6

Printed and bound in the United States of America

QG 9 8 7 6 5 4 3 2 1

CONTENTS

INTRODUCTION

This is a book about home cooking. It's about real food. And it's about easy. But it's not speed cooking. In fact, at first glance a dozen ingredients in a recipe may not look easy, but here's the secret: it's the electric pressure cooker (EPC). If you put the ingredients into the pot the way we've outlined in each recipe, you'll get a finished product that will advance your culinary capabilities. We've made it easy for you to serve your family chef-at-home-quality meals without needing 20-plus years of experience in a professional kitchen. We did that part for you. We've taken many classics, requiring many different skill sets and techniques, and squeezed them all into the electric pressure cooker. We lovingly refer to our home pressure cooker as the "meal machine." But let's back things up a bit.

We met working in the kitchen in our youth, back when we were "jung und spritzig." These days, we are two well-trained chefs with a growing, hungry family and a freelance lifestyle. We cook from scratch at home with simple ingredients and try to get the best vegetables and proteins we can afford. Cooking for and feeding the rascals, as well as ourselves, is a huge part of our lives. We have a small garden, and each year we try to grow a few tomatoes and cucumbers, lots of herbs, and a few rows of lettuce. Admittedly, we're not great farmers. That's fine – we have fun, the kids are into it, and we're happy to support the local markets. We squeeze five of us around the family table every day, and there's always room for guests.

One day while pondering the meal plan, we were throwing around ideas on how we could make things a little easier, a little faster within our tight schedule. A friend suggested an EPC. Although we're not the type for kitchen gimmicks, the next thing you know, there's an electric pressure cooker in our house. Admittedly, it sat in the box for over a week. We'd smile at it, wondering what to do with it. We knew only of the horror stories from our elders, but out of the box it finally came. Manual read, water test done. Let's do this.

Not long after we started cooking with the electric pressure cooker, we noticed that the flavours were different, in a good way: there was far more flavour – and better flavour – than we expected. This pressure cooker was no gimmick – not just another countertop appliance. This was the real deal. We had perfectly cooked chickpeas, creamy on the inside with a tender pop when you bite in. They had such a wonderful clean flavour. Next was the day of the carrots. "You have to try these carrots, Mia! They taste like . . . *carrots!*" Regular grocery store carrots these were, but bursting with enough robust flavour to make an impression. We had not had a more carroty experience in all our years of cooking and eating. We were hooked. We wanted to cook everything in our pressure cooker. After a few more weeks of meals, we were learning the ins and the outs of the machine. We discovered that it was superb at soups, stews, and braises, which would normally take two or even three times as long to prepare on the stovetop. And the flavours were notably intense.

For this book, we approached the electric pressure cooker as if it were the only heat source we had in our kitchen. If this machine was designed to do all it promised, we wouldn't need the others. We've designed these recipes exclusively for the EPC. We always pressure cook and sauté on high, and set the timer using the manual controls. It makes these recipes easy to follow and really simplifies the machine operation. While sometimes they have different names, these settings are pretty standard across the popular brands of EPCs.

We know that, in the real world, many people have more than just the EPC and choose to bake, broil, or grill items before or after pressure cooking to get the finish and texture they like. Go ahead – have fun and do it your way. That being said, you won't find recipes in this book that require frying pans, barbecues, ovens, or microwaves. You and your machine, just the two of you, can go a long way together.

When we started cooking with an electric pressure cooker, and because of the hype, we were excited for all the time we were going to save but unaware of the other benefits that soon came to light. It was after we made beef stock (page 138) and veal osso buco (page 159) in the same afternoon that we realized how the machine could change the way we cooked meals at home. Pre-EPC, a couple of pots simmering on the stove for the better part of a day would have our windows steamed up and our air conditioner battling to keep up. We knew then that, even if our meals took the same amount of time to prepare in the electric pressure cooker as they do on the stove (which they certainly don't), we would be tempted to use the pressure cooker just for the economy we were getting elsewhere.

In that spirit, we worked our machine hard for this book. We pushed it to its limits just to see where they were. We found them and, yes, we messed up a few meals in the process. First it was the Cuban black beans (page 67), which were a limp, watery failure. But we tinkered with the recipe and now it shines. Then it was a misconceived rigatoni recipe, so bad it wasn't salvageable. Thus began our quest for a truly good pasta dish, which we found in the macaroni and cheese (page 93). The first attempt at goulash in the EPC ended up burned to the bottom, a classic case of not enough water. There were two attempts at gumbo that set off the machine's safety sensors, shutting it down. We shelved the idea for some time, until we considered making a separate roux (page 19) to thicken it up after the cook rather than before. Just like that, we had gumbo again, which morphed its way to a spectacular jambalaya instead (page 224). It was like learning to cook anew. These hurdles led to stronger recipes as we pushed forward, further modifying techniques and understanding that being incredibly specific with the amount of liquid in each recipe led to better outcomes. Bringing thicker, tomato-based dishes to a simmer before closing the lid, allowing for much less time between the last stir and the start of the pressure cycle, was another lesson we learned the hard way. Same goes for some of the recipes high in sugar, with that ingredient now often added at the end as a safeguard against burning. We learned to replace large amounts of low-fat dairy with small amounts of the high-fat variety. Many times, there's already enough liquid when you remove the lid, so all you need is the creaminess. And on and on. We were never afraid to go back to the drawing board.

Let's face it: recent generations were brought up scared of pressure cookers, and that's the main reason they fell out of fashion after the 1960s – although it's not the only reason. Dig a little into the history of food and you can see other influences at play during that era. Food-processing technology was advancing, and the proliferation of frozen foods and convenience items such as the TV dinner were gaining popularity. There was a sea change. People left the scary mechanical apparatus in the cupboard, opting for the safe, clean speediness of convenience foods. With the general acceptance of the countertop microwave in the late 1970s, convenience officially had a stranglehold on our food and our flavour. But new generations are discovering that big flavour is cool again. With the breakthrough invention of the electric pressure cooker, we can have safety, convenience, *and* flavour! Let's take flavour back. Get your electric pressure cooker out of the box, run the water test, and let's get cooking. For real.

BEFORE YOU BEGIN

How Do I Use This Thing?

Good news: using an electric pressure cooker (EPC) doesn't have to be complicated. We cut through all the clutter and the presets and focus on only a few of the buttons. This book uses the following methods:

- Simply throw all ingredients inside and close the lid.
- Sauté ingredients in the open pot and then close the lid.
- Throw ingredients in the pot to cook, and use the sauté function *after* you've removed the lid.

Sometimes you'll release the steam right away, and sometimes you'll wait a few minutes more, to let the contents of the pot continue to cook while the pot cools down. But that's really all there is to it. Easy!

Safety First

Instant Favourites isn't meant for your grandma's pressure cooker. The fact is, you wouldn't be reading this book if it weren't for the advancement of the safety features typical of today's pressure cookers.

So to answer a few of your likely concerns, here are some of the ways today's electric pressure cooker keeps you out of danger (read your manual for specifics about your machine):

- The lid locks in place and cannot be removed while contents are under pressure.
- The machine can detect when there's too much pressure in the pot and automatically releases steam to compensate.
- If the pot overheats, the machine will throttle the heater and basically shut down.
- If food is burning on the bottom, the machine will not come to pressure. If that happens, remove the lid, use a flat-ended wooden spoon to release any food stuck to the bottom, and try again. You may also need to add a little more liquid.

Keep your seal in place, the lid clean, and the valves clear of debris and you shouldn't have any problems.

Natural Release versus Quick Release

One of the first concepts to understand is the difference between the electric pressure cooker's two release methods: natural and quick. Natural release is very gentle compared to the quick release.

Natural Release

Full natural release is allowing the machine to cool on its own. After the pressure cooking cycle has finished and the heating element is off, you let the machine sit until it cools down to the point where it's no longer under pressure. The contents will have cooled from over 250°F (120°C) to 212°F (100°C). The more you have in the pot, the longer it will take to fully cool – anywhere from 10 minutes for something like quinoa to 2 hours or more for stocks. Remember, the food is still under pressure until the pin drops down, and therefore continues to cook at a temperature hotter than boiling water. Although in some ways the natural release method is similar to a "resting" phase, it's a misnomer to call it that. You aren't resting anything until you take the lid off. You are, in fact, continuing to cook, although at a gradually decreasing pressure level.

To get the right amount of heat over time, and to reach the desired texture and consistency, you'll often need to use an initial natural release before completely depressurizing the pot. These times are calculated into the cooking times. If you quick release when you should natural release, you're going to have a bad time. Follow the recipe. You may want that stew or roast right now, but let it finish cooking or it will be undercooked, sacrificing flavour and tenderness.

Quick Release

The quick release method goes like this: you trigger the machine's pressure release function right after the pressure cooking cycle, or after a designated amount of natural release time. On some models, this is a button you push to make the machine do it; others have a toggle switch or valve, which you manually change from sealed to venting. This is the part that frightens people about pressure cookers. When you flip the valve from sealed to vent, you get a show. A loud, powerful stream of steam jets out through the valve, so stand back. After you've experienced it a time or two, it won't be a big deal. In fact, it will become your new dinner bell.

What's Happening Inside?

So, you've closed the lid and set the timer. What's going on in there? The liquid starts to boil, creating water vapour – also known as steam. This process continues at a vigorous rate, and the steam can't escape the pot. The water vapour fills the pot, yet the machine continues to generate steam, further filling the pot and creating pressure. What happens next is an example of Gay-Lussac's Law, which states that temperature and pressure are directly proportional to each other. When pressure increases, temperature increases – and that's exactly what happens inside the pot. Pressure and temperature continue to increase to 1 bar, or about 15 psi, creating temperatures of about 250°F (120°C).

At the point when the timer starts, the vapour and the liquid are in equilibrium. The empty space in the pot is so full of water vapour that boiling can't even occur – aside from a small simmer while vapour and liquid exchange places, remaining in equilibrium. Because of its excited state, the vapour pushes itself onto all surfaces. This action continues until the machine is shut off and allowed to cool completely, or the release valve is triggered. In a quick release scenario, you have water vapour escaping through the valve, ultimately making space for more water vapour inside the pot. The liquids will begin to boil rapidly again until the temperature drops below 212°F (100°C), coinciding with the full release of pressure. Although this rapid-boil finish is no problem in many recipes, and in fact is necessary for quite a few, some foods should not be quick released

because of it. Beans, grains, jams, and other foods that tend to foam during boiling should not be quick released right after the pressure cooking cycle because the foamy bubbles will reach the vent and sputter through, spraying everywhere and creating quite a mess. If this happens to you, close the valve and try again in 5 or 10 minutes. It occurs more frequently when the pot is full and the surface of the liquid is closer to the top, where the vent is located.

Managing Moisture

One of the challenges to pressure cooking is managing the moisture content because the amount of water you put in is the amount of water you get out. That means no reducing or natural thickening by evaporation occurs.

When you remove the lid on the machine, the underside will be covered in water droplets formed during the cook. The machine has a reservoir for this liquid, which drains into a removable cup – making it easier to discard. When you remove the lid, direct that liquid into the reservoir, rather than having it drip into the pot. There's nothing wrong with that liquid. It's just more water you don't need in your tomato sauce or your rice. It's a little thing. But, hey, you went through all that work, why not make your dishes the best they can possibly be?

Read the Manual

Finally, before we move on to some notes about the recipes and their ingredients, here's a reminder to read the manual. We can't stress this point enough. It's not too long of a read, and you'll be a happier cook when you understand what's going on with your pot. Most brands recommend that you run a water test first, where you simply add a cup or two of water to the pot, secure the lid, and run a short pressure cooking cycle. This test allows you to get acquainted with the user interface and see how the machine works before getting serious with actual meals. It takes some of the mystery out of pressure cooking and is a great way to encourage you to take the machine out of the box and get started.

NOTES FOR THE COOK

We're not here to tell you how to live your life, in the kitchen or anywhere else, but we can make suggestions based on our experience with the EPC.

Shoulders, shanks, general stewing meat, and chicken thighs are all electric pressure cooker friendly. The pressure cooker is amazing for soups, stews, and braises. Cooking pulses, such as dried beans, is also a breeze. We wouldn't dare cook a steak in the electric pressure cooker – that's what grills and cast iron pans are for.

About the Recipes

Most of the recipes in this book are designed for instant gratification, although some, such as the sauces and condiments, are intended for later use. There are also a handful of recipes that can benefit from a full cool down and reheat before serving, permitting more water vapour to escape and allowing flavours to develop. It's a personal preference.

Soup Today, Stew Tomorrow

How many times have you had the same chili or stew the next day and wondered why it tastes better? Recipes like those for our cheeseburger soup (page 115) or Hungarian beef goulash (page 157) actually benefit from cooling completely and being reheated

when you're hungry. Every dish you make in the EPC will thicken as it cools. Sometimes that's a good thing, and sometimes it's not. Breakfast strata jars (page 257) and mushroom and spinach risotto (page 100) are both best eaten right after they're made. Cabbage roll soup (page 119) becomes cabbage roll stew a day later, and it's just as delicious. If you're reheating soups and stews and prefer them the way they came out of the pot, add a little water – that's all you're missing.

Why the Flavours Are So Intense – the Maillard Reaction

As food scientists explore the molecules that make up flavour and aroma, there's been a lot of buzz about the Maillard reaction – the chemical reaction that gives roasted meats, and other foods, their signature colour and flavour. This reaction can occur at room temperature, but it really gets moving at high heats – about 250°F (120°C) and above. These temperatures are attainable in the electric pressure cooker and are most evident in stocks and dishes with longer cooking times, such as beef carnitas (page 155). Just remember, each ingredient reacts to heat in its own way, and some ingredients react more than others.

The Maillard reaction, simplified, is a series of reactions between sugars and amino acids in your food, creating complex flavour and aroma molecules still being studied by food scientists. The reaction is responsible for some of the intense flavours you get from the EPC, and you can see evidence of it in your everyday cooking in the telltale browning and pleasant aromas of seared meats, toasted bread, and roasted coffee. This reaction differs from caramelization, which results from sugars breaking down when heated.

Different foodstuffs contain distinct sugars and a variety of amino acids at varying levels. The effects of the Maillard reaction are not as notable in pulses and rice but are particularly notable in tomatoes, carrots, and meats. It's also what makes condensed milk turn from a creamy white to a rich brown colour in dulce de leche (page 267).

Planning

In this book, we're not going to trick you into a "10-minute recipe" only to frustrate you after 45 minutes of cooking. Too many online recipes will bait you into clicking by telling you only the pressure cooking time, leaving the details of prep, pressurizing, and depressurizing slyly out of view. Read the full recipe before starting; the timing is all very clear.

Good food takes planning, and that's what the recipes in this book demand. You want to be prepared before you hit the start button. Have all your ingredients ready or, as the cool kids say, your *mise en place* – your "meez." Things move pretty fast once you start, and you want to be ready. Focus on getting all the things into the pot, and then secure the lid and go about your business while you wait for the timer. Sourcing and gathering ingredients take time, and cutting, chopping, and cleaning up are all time-consuming, too. The machine makes the cooking part fairly quick and easy. Once you close the lid, you'll have a cutting board, a knife, and some peripheral items to clean, and later the pot itself.

Sourcing Ingredients

Thanks to the Internet, it's never been easier to locate ingredients and find the right stores. International food stores dot the map. Some cities are obviously more populated with a mix of cultures, and that's where you'll find a greater variety of shops. In the area in and around Toronto, where we live, we have access to products from all over the world.

No matter where you are, you can bring the world to your kitchen. If you can't find a particular chili pepper, feel free to substitute another. And if you're missing a suggested fresh herb, feel free to experiment. When in doubt, dig a little deeper – those ingredients may be closer than you think.

About the Ingredients

In developing the recipes for this book, we've carefully chosen ingredients based on those best suited to the electric pressure cooker. Here are some general rules and guidelines to follow for best results.

Soak the Beans – Period

The recipes in this book call for soaked dried beans – white beans, black beans, or garbanzo beans (a.k.a. chickpeas). Here's how you do it.

Rinse the dried beans in cold running water and place them in a container large enough to hold at least twice their volume. Fill the container with at least twice the amount of water as beans (2 parts water to 1 part beans). The beans will expand to double the size as they absorb the water. Refrigerate at least 12 hours but ideally for 24 hours. (We usually cover the container to prevent spills and to keep the water clean.)

Before soaking   After 24 hours

Drain and rinse the beans before cooking.

So, why do we do it this way? What's the point? Besides the fact that the recipes in this book won't work if you don't soak your beans, there are specific benefits to the process. Properly soaked beans will

- keep their shape better once cooked
- have a texture superior to canned or unsoaked beans
- be easier to digest
- cook faster (that's why we're here, right?)

Soaking beans takes only a moment of your time. Keep a variety of dried beans in your pantry and you'll be more likely to soak them for tomorrow's dinner. Once you start, you won't go back.

Dried beans require a minimum 12-hour soak to be considered "soaked." Twenty-four hours of soaking is ideal and, if your beans happen to soak for 36–48 hours, you can still use them. However, after 48 hours, the beans will either start to sprout or to smell as they slowly begin to ferment – and that's not recommended for the recipes in this book.

One final point: there's nothing wrong with canned beans, but be aware that most common brands have added salt plus calcium chloride (a no-sodium salt and firming agent) and, in some cases, other additives. If you soak and cook the beans yourself, you control the salt and you don't need any preservatives. So if you want maximum control, flavour, and nutrition, it makes sense to make food from scratch.

Avoid Cooking from Frozen

While experimenting with the machine in the early part of our time together, one thing we found puzzling at first, but which made a whole bunch of sense later on, was something we do when making large batches of stock on the stovetop. After accumulating scraps and bones of beef and pork in our freezer, we would empty them, still frozen, into a stock pot, cover them with water, and simmer for hours. We never had a problem. One day we tried the same method in the machine – and did have a problem. Although the cooking liquid did come to a boil and the pot was pressurized initially, the mostly still-frozen meat and bones cooled it down to a point where it was no longer hot enough in the pot to keep the pressure. The machine took this as a sign of something wrong – that it was malfunctioning in some way – and turned itself off.

So thaw all frozen meat before cooking. There's nothing wrong with frozen foods, but keep in mind that water tends to leach from meat during the thaw. This added moisture will affect the recipes, thinning out flavours and producing watery results.

A Note about Salt

We use Diamond brand kosher salt in our kitchen and throughout the book. The company doesn't pay us anything – we just like the feel of this salt. It's light and airy, and not abrasive in any way. If you use regular iodized table salt in these recipes, you'll need to cut the amount of salt by about half. Table salt is much finer and more dense; therefore, more of it will fit in a measuring spoon. Sea salt and fancy salts from around the world will also need to be used with caution.

Many recipes call for salt at the start of the preparation, where you need to sauté vegetables right away. This salting is important because it helps to draw moisture out of the vegetables more efficiently. If you're cutting back on salt, still add some in these instances. Bottom line: season to taste. When in doubt, add a pinch of salt and taste the results. Add a little at a time until you reach your bliss point. Then stop, before you get addicted!

Let's Address Thickeners

Fresh produce and meats are made of water – about 75%–95% for vegetables and 65%–75% for meat. So a recipe using fresh ingredients will never turn out exactly the same way twice. We use thickeners to capture the flavours, bring all the juices together, and create a pleasant "mouth feel."

Cornstarch is, hands down, the easiest way to thicken soups and sauces. It's widely available and easy to work with. Here's how you use it. Place the cornstarch into a small dish and add some water – about 1 tbsp cornstarch to 1–2 tbsp water. You want it to be easy enough to mix together but not too watery, since we *are* trying to thicken here.

Cornstarch should be added to simmering or boiling liquid and be whisked in slowly to avoid lumps. Add half the cornstarch and evaluate the effect before adding more. Keep in mind that everything thickens as it cools.

If you're inclined, consider making a classic French roux (page 19). While you're not using the electric pressure cooker for pressurizing, you can use the sauté function to make roux for many dishes in this book, such as leg of lamb with white wine gravy (page 213), meat lover's chili (page 141), and stuffed turkey dinner (page 201).

A Note about Butter

Salted versus unsalted butter? In our kitchen, we use unsalted butter by default. We do a fair amount of baking and, by using only unsalted, we never have to guess which butter is out at the time. The recipes in this book call for unsalted butter unless otherwise stated. You can also use your EPC to make a clarified butter known as ghee (page 17). We use ghee in many recipes that require sautéing and where we believe the flavour is a good fit for the dish.

Canned and Jarred Tomatoes

You'll find four types of processed tomatoes in this book, each variety chosen specifically for the recipe it appears in. They all have different moisture levels and offer unique textures. The most common vessel is the 28-oz (796 ml) can.

Canned tomatoes have many advantages. For instance, they are

- very consistent in flavour and moisture content
- packed in season for best flavour
- inexpensive and widely available year-round

This makes canned a better choice for the EPC than fresh in many instances.

Whole tomatoes. Whole tomatoes are great for when you want large pieces of tomato in the finished dish. These can be hand crushed to the desired consistency or puréed. This style of tomato contains the least amount of water of all the varieties.

Crushed tomatoes. Crushed tomatoes are excellent for sauces and thicker-style soups. They are roughly the same texture as a puréed can of whole tomatoes.

Passata. It's much like crushed tomatoes, but passata is slightly thinner in texture because it's strained. Passata often comes in jars that contain about 3 cups of tomato.

Canned diced tomatoes. Use diced tomatoes in brothy soups, when you want small pieces of tomato without the tomato sauce look. This style of tomato contains the most water.

Hot Peppers

On a scale of 1–6, from mildest to hottest, these are the hot peppers you'll find in the recipes (see photo on page 15):

1. poblano
2. jalapeño
3. finger chili
4. serrano
5. red or green Thai bird chili
6. Scotch bonnet/habanero

Most of the heat within any hot pepper is in the seeds, where the bulk of the capsaicin component is found. The decision to include or remove the seeds is yours. For more heat, leave the seeds in. For a more mild heat, remove them. You can also opt to put a whole uncut or un-pierced chili pepper into soups or stews to give flavour and subtle heat to the dish. Just remove the pepper before serving. It's important to handle hot peppers safely. The seeds are the potent portion, but a pepper's skin and flesh have enough capsaicin to cause discomfort if handled improperly during prep. For setting up the most effective barrier between food and skin, use rubber gloves when handling peppers – especially a large amount of them. Carefully and thoroughly washing your hands with soap and water should suffice for casual contact. Just be vigilant about avoiding any contact between hands and eyes or other sensitive body parts.

poblano

red and green
Thai bird chili

jalapeño

Scotch bonnet/
habanero

red finger chili

serrano

Herbs

Using fresh herbs is one of the chef's best tricks. There's no substitute for fresh, so use them with abandon in the summer and chop and freeze them for the rest of the year. Dried herbs have their place, but nothing can compare with the powerful flavours that fresh herbs provide. Here's how to handle and store fresh herbs.

The best strategy is to have a small herb garden and pick as you need. Then, harvest the lot in the fall for processing and freezing. But not everyone is into gardening – even windowsill gardening – so you may need to purchase herbs from time to time, especially in colder climates. Here's a brief guide.

Basil. Basil is one of the most fragile of herbs and works well as an indoor potted plant. If you buy bunches of fresh basil, wrap them in plastic and store in the warmest part of the fridge, away from the fan. Exposure to very cold temperatures will wilt the herb and turn the basil to an unappetizing black. If you need to extend the life of your basil, blend the leaves with a little olive oil in a food processor and store in the refrigerator for a week or in the freezer for up to 3 months.

Parsley, cilantro, tarragon, and other tender-leaf herbs. The members of this group of herbs are best when washed and spun in a salad spinner before storing in the refrigerator for up to a week. Line a sealable container or freezer bag with a damp paper towel and place the herbs inside it. If you need to keep the herbs longer, chop them finely and mix in about a quarter-cup of olive oil for each cup of chopped herbs; then freeze the mixture in flexible silicone ice cube trays. When you need them, use the herb cubes, still frozen, in recipes. You may want to keep a designated herb tray for this purpose since herbs tend to leave a lingering flavour that may affect regular ice cubes. (You don't want cilantro in your Scotch on the rocks.)

Rosemary, oregano, sage, and thyme. These herbs, the sturdiest of them all, have intense flavours. They're best stored unwashed in plastic wrap or a tight sealing container. They can be frozen whole and used directly from the freezer without thawing. You'll know they're starting to expire when they start to go brown.

Ghee

Ghee is butter that has had the milk simmered away, leaving a distinct nutty flavour. It has a high smoke point, which makes it great for frying since it remains unscathed by temperatures as high as 482°F (250°C), after which the molecules start to break down. A staple in Indian cuisine, ghee is gaining popularity and is now available at many grocery stores. It is shelf stable until you open the package – then it needs to be refrigerated to avoid rancidity.

Set the machine to sauté and add the butter.

Allow the butter to melt. Simmer for about 4–5 minutes, stirring frequently to prevent scorching.

Turn off the machine and allow the melted butter to cool slightly before passing it through a fine sieve. There should be no "water" or milk left – only oil. Some milk solids will have adhered to the bottom of the pot during the process. That's all right since you don't want that part anyway.

Store ghee, covered and refrigerated, for up to 3 months.

1 lb unsalted butter

Roux

A traditional French all-purpose thickener, roux is made by combining butter and flour at a ratio of 1:1 by weight – in other words, half butter and half flour. The mixture is then heated to "cook out" the flour taste and give the flour a light brown colour. It's ready to use after it's cooled. Used mostly at the end of cooking, the roux should be whisked into sauces a little at a time to avoid lumps and over-thickening.

½ lb unsalted butter, cubed
½ lb (about 1½ cups) all-purpose flour

Add the butter and flour to the pot and set the machine to sauté.

Stir the mixture frequently while the butter melts and begins to combine with the flour. Use a flat-ended wooden spoon to make sure it doesn't stick to the bottom. Continue this process for about 10 minutes or until the flour begins to brown lightly. Carefully remove the pot from the machine to stop the cooking process.

Allow to cool. Cover and refrigerate for up to 2 months.

Notes: The roux will go hard in the fridge, like butter does.

This amount makes enough roux for at least a dozen recipes.

This recipe is easily halved or doubled. Smaller amounts will cook a few minutes faster, and larger amounts will take a few more minutes.

You can also freeze the roux. When it has cooled to room temperature, divide into tablespoon amounts and freeze for up to a year. (You can use a silicone ice cube tray and then transfer the portions to sealable bags.)

Spices

We use a mortar and pestle as well as a spice grinder for grinding up fresh whole spices. We prefer whole spices because they keep their flavour longer than pre-ground versions, and they're easier to identify when they jostle for space in the spice cupboard. We store our spices in a cool, dark place in sealed containers or jars. It's best to buy small amounts and use them up rather than letting them get old.

Useful Tools

A number of tools are particularly helpful for use with the electric pressure cooker and are specifically called for in the recipes in the book. Keep them close at hand.

Flat-Ended Wooden Spoon

This is your best friend when it comes to cooking up dishes in the electric pressure cooker. It gives you the power to scrape the bottom of the pot without the aggressiveness or abrasiveness of metal. The flat edge makes it perfect for ensuring nothing sticks to the bottom of the pot.

Garam masala before grinding

Garam masala after grinding

Hand Blender

The hand blender, also known as an immersion blender or a stick blender, allows you to purée or blend ingredients right in the pot. There's no need to transfer hot liquids in batches to a countertop blender or food processor.

Measuring Cups, Measuring Spoons, and a Kitchen Scale

Accurate measurements lead to scrumptious results. Try the recipes as written before tweaking any measurements. Having the right amount of liquid is key to your success.

Kitchen scales are not as popular as they should be, but they're incredibly handy.

Steamer Basket

Steamer baskets are great tools for simple steaming. They work a bit like the trivet that comes with the electric pressure cooker in that they keep the food suspended over the liquid in the bottom of the pot. The main difference is that a steamer's finer openings allow the basket to hold smaller items.

Canning Tongs

If you prepare a lot of recipes in individual jars or ramekins, these tongs will make your life a lot easier, and safer, when trying to remove hot items after cooking.

Garlic Press and Rasp/Microplane Grater

Oh, the time we've saved thanks to the garlic press. A great way to mince garlic in a hurry, it does a pretty good job on ginger, too.

The rasp or microplane grater is another wonderful tool. It originated in the woodshop before chefs discovered its power to finely zest lemons and limes, and grate ginger, Parmesan cheese, nutmeg, and even garlic.

Ladles

If you don't already have several different-sized ladles, pick up a few. They make it easy when your meal is ready to serve.

Canning Jars, Ramekins, and Silicone Baking Cups

Have some fun with your machine, and try a few "pot in pot" recipes such as pots de crème (page 241) and breakfast strata jars (page 257). Make sure the receptacles are oven safe before using them. Remember, every time glass jars get banged about, they weaken – and they can occasionally crack under pressure. Inspect glass canning jars before use for small cracks, which can become big cracks after the rigours of a pressure cooker cycle. If you make canning jar recipes a lot, you may want to invest in metal or silicone cups for durability.

Cake Pans

Small cake pans also work well inside the machine. For examples of how to use this method of cooking, see the carrot cake (page 251) or the one-pot salmon dinner (page 227). A solid one-piece cake pan works well for things that have a tendency to leak out of springform pans.

Mortar and Pestle

It's one of the oldest kitchen tools that still has a place in today's modernized cooking environment. The mortar (the heavy bowl) and the pestle (the solid, blunt grinding implement) have been used since early civilization for grinding grains and seeds, making them easier to eat. In this book, we use it for grinding whole spices. The flavour of freshly ground whole spices is better, stronger, and more pronounced, much like freshly ground coffee has a richer, rounder flavour and is considered superior to pre-ground. Ours at home is a medium-sized version made out of granite. It has a little texture to it, which the spices catch on, speeding up the grinding process. Some of the rougher textured mortar and pestles should be seasoned first by grinding a small amount of raw rice, which will encourage any loose bits of stone to fall out into the rice. Discard the rice and wash the mortar and pestle with water. Always make sure it is dried well before storing, and use soap on it only if you have to.

Fat-Skimming Techniques

There are a few different ways to remove the fat that sometimes settles on top of the liquid in your pot after cooking. Sometimes it's just a little fat that you want to stir in, but other times there's just too much of it. Saucy pulled pork (page 177) and Korean-inspired short ribs (page 153) are good examples of recipes that benefit when you take the time to remove the layer of fat before finishing the sauce. Here are a few ways to accomplish this job:

Paper towels. Carefully but quickly drag a paper towel across the surface of the fat, allowing it to absorb the grease. Repeat with fresh paper towels until you've removed as much fat as you wish.

Ladle. Use a ladle to spoon off the top layer of fat. Make a small swirling motion using only the bottom of the ladle to encourage the fat to move toward the edges of the pot. Then, holding the ladle mostly level with the surface, move it around the edge of the pot, allowing only the fat to enter the ladle. Discard the fat and repeat as necessary.

Fat separator. This is a measuring cup–style vessel with a spout extending from the bottom, mostly associated with gravy making. Pour the liquid into the cup and allow it to settle. The fat will float and will not be able to move into the spout, so simply pour off the good stuff and leave the fat in the cup.

Refrigerator. This technique requires time, but it works very well. Refrigerate the liquid, and once the contents have chilled, the floating fat solidifies, making it very easy to remove.

Enjoy Your Pot

We enjoy our speedy and economical electric pressure cooker – our "meal machine" – and we've taken pleasure in sharing our recipes and methods with you. We hope you use *Instant Favourites* as a valuable resource for flavour combinations and flavour-building techniques, and even as a reference for cook times once you start venturing out on your own, coming up with new recipes to share with family and friends. Get ready for real food, keep your manual handy, and don't forget to soak your beans.

Zippy Jalapeño and Ginger Hot Sauce

DIPS AND HOT SAUCES

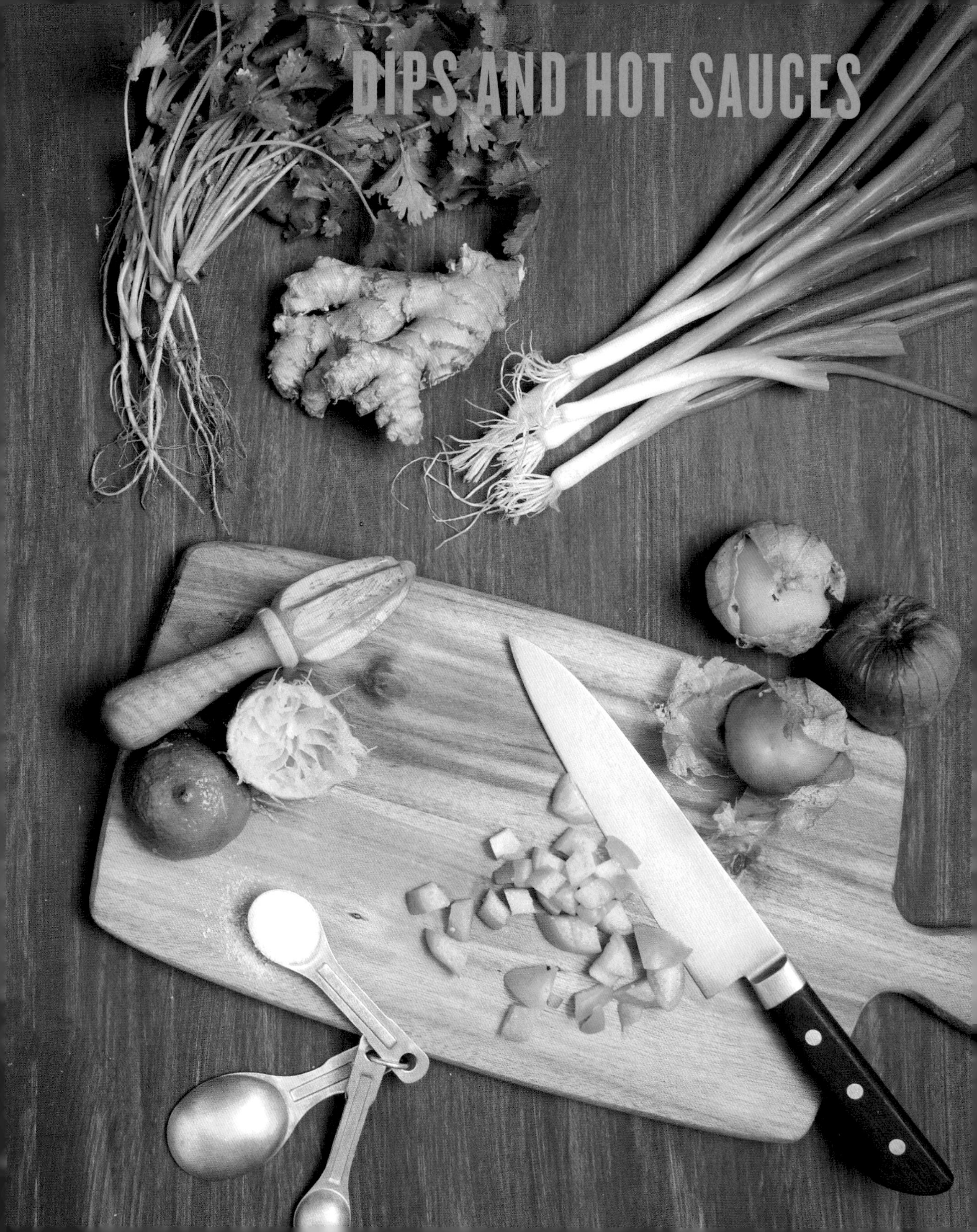

White Bean and Garlic Confit Dip

This is such a smooth and creamy dip for snacking on with fresh-cut vegetables or flatbreads such as pita. White bean dip can do anything hummus can do, and it's nice to switch it up once in a while. Make a batch for the week, if it will last that long.

Place the dried white beans into a container large enough to hold double the volume. Cover with 4 cups of water and refrigerate for a minimum of 12 hours, although 24 hours is ideal.

Drain and rinse the soaked white beans and add them to the pot with the 2 cups of water, bay leaf, thyme, salt, and 1 tbsp of olive oil. Secure the lid.

Set the machine for 10 minutes on high pressure. Allow for a 10-minute natural release before completely depressurizing the pot.

Remove the lid and add the lemon juice, garlic confit, and 3 tbsp of olive oil. Stir to combine. Cool to room temperature before removing the thyme sprigs and bay leaf and blending with a hand blender right in the pot.

Refrigerate until needed. Serve sprinkled with chopped fresh chives.

Makes 6 cups

Notes: This recipe is easily halved.

If making garlic confit is not in the cards, 6–8 peeled garlic cloves cooked in with the beans will work. Alternatively, 2–3 peeled garlic cloves, minced and added at the mixing stage, will give you the garlic flavour you need.

2 cups dried white beans

2 cups water

1 bay leaf

2 sprigs fresh thyme

1 tbsp kosher salt

1 tbsp olive oil

1 lemon, juiced (about ¼ cup)

**2 tbsp garlic confit
(page 81 or see Note)**

3 tbsp olive oil

¼ cup chopped fresh chives

Baba Ganoush

Baba ganoush. It tastes great, and it's fun to say. This dip gets its texture from the ultra-soft eggplant and much of its flavour from the tahini, a nutty, earthy-tasting paste made of finely ground sesame seeds. If your tahini separates, this isn't a problem. Just give it a good stir, and all is well again.

In a large bowl, mix together the garlic, olive oil, water, lemon juice, and salt.

Add the eggplant to the bowl and turn or toss to evenly coat all sides in the juice. Allow to sit 10–15 minutes, turning once after 2–3 minutes.

Place the eggplant with the marinade into the pot.

Secure the lid and set the machine for 4 minutes on high pressure. Allow for a 5-minute natural release before completely depressurizing the pot.

Remove the lid and use a wooden spoon to mash up the eggplant while stirring in the tahini.

Allow the baba ganoush to cool, uncovered, before refrigerating. Stir it once in a while to help it cool faster and allow more moisture to escape.

Makes 2 cups

4 cloves garlic, chopped

¼ cup olive oil

2 tbsp water

1 lemon, juiced (about ¼ cup)

1 tsp kosher salt

1 medium eggplant, peeled and sliced into ½-inch rounds

⅓ cup tahini

Eggplant Raita

Raita is an Indian condiment that's basically the opposite of hot sauce. It's perfect to serve with robust, spicy dishes and curries because of its cool and soothing effect. The electric pressure cooker breaks down the eggplant so well, you don't even need a food processor for this recipe.

Place the yogurt into a fine sieve over a bowl and allow it to drain, uncovered, in the refrigerator for 24 hours. The yogurt will lose about 1 cup of liquid, making it much thicker.

Cut the top and bottom off the eggplant and peel. Discard end pieces and skin.

Slice the eggplant lengthwise through the centre and cut into ½-inch-thick semicircles.

In a bowl, place the eggplant, olive oil, water, lemon juice, and salt and toss to coat evenly. Set aside for 10–15 minutes to allow the eggplant to absorb some of the flavours and release some moisture.

Place the marinated eggplant and all the residual marinade into the pressure cooker and secure the lid.

Set the machine to high pressure for 4 minutes. Allow for a 5-minute natural release before completely depressurizing the pot.

Remove the lid and use a wooden spoon to stir the eggplant vigorously and mash it up. Remove from the pot to cool to room temperature.

Stir in the strained yogurt and the chopped basil and mint. Season with salt and freshly ground black pepper.

Cover and refrigerate for up to a week. Serve with a drizzle of olive oil on top.

Makes 2 cups

2 cups plain full-fat yogurt

1 medium eggplant

2 tbsp olive oil

2 tbsp water

½ lemon, juiced (2 tbsp)

1 tsp kosher salt

1 tbsp chopped fresh basil

½ tbsp chopped fresh mint

salt and freshly ground
    black pepper

Classic Hummus

This recipe is easy, especially if you have a hand blender. Everything happens in the pot, so cleanup is minimal. There's precisely the right amount of water in the recipe, so no need to strain the chickpeas once they're cooked. Just remove the lid, add the rest of the ingredients, and blend. You'll have a sturdy dip to take on the road, serve as a snack for growing kids, or dress up and bring out for cocktails.

Place the dried chickpeas into a container large enough to hold double the volume. Cover with 4 cups of water and refrigerate for a minimum of 12 hours, although 24 hours is ideal.

Drain and rinse the soaked chickpeas and add them to the pot with the 2 cups of water, 2 tsp of salt, and the 1 tbsp of olive oil. Secure the lid.

Set the machine for 20 minutes on high pressure. Allow for a 10-minute natural release before completely depressurizing the pot.

Remove the lid and add the garlic. Roughly blend with a hand blender, making sure the garlic gets broken up.

Add the ½ cup of olive oil, along with the lemon juice, tahini, and 2–3 tsp of salt, and continue to blend with the hand blender. You may have to remove the inner pot from the cooker and tilt it to one side so the blades of the blender are submerged.

The hummus will thicken as it cools. Stir in a tablespoon or so of water to adjust the consistency if desired.

Once at room temperature, the hummus is ready to eat. If you want to take this dip to the next level, spoon the desired amount of hummus onto a plate or into a shallow bowl, drizzle with olive oil, and sprinkle with chopped fresh parsley and a dash of paprika.

Serve with naan bread, crackers, or fresh vegetables for dipping.

Makes 6 cups

Note: This recipe is easily halved.

2 cups dried chickpeas
2 cups water
2 tsp kosher salt
1 tbsp olive oil
5 large cloves garlic
½ cup olive oil
2 lemons, juiced (about ½ cup)
⅓ cup tahini
2–3 tsp kosher salt
olive oil, chopped fresh
** parsley, paprika**
** (optional garnishes)**

Zippy Jalapeño and Ginger Hot Sauce

In this sauce, based on a simple salsa verde, the ginger brightens the flavour and intensifies the heat. Bring it out on taco night for those who like it hot. It also works well if you want to spice up your tortilla soup (page 129) or pork pozole (page 163).

Place all the ingredients into the pot. Place the pot into the machine, and secure the lid.

Set the machine for 10 minutes on high pressure. Once the pressure cooking cycle has finished, depressurize completely using the quick release method.

Remove the lid and use a hand blender to purée the sauce right in the pot.

Cool to room temperature before transferring to sealable containers or jars and refrigerating for up to 3 months.

Makes 1½ cups

Note: This recipe is easily doubled.

8 jalapeño peppers, stems removed, cut in half lengthwise

5 green onions, roughly chopped

2 tomatillos, husks removed, washed, and roughly diced

2 inches fresh ginger, peeled and cut into ¼-inch coins

1 bunch fresh cilantro, roots removed

1 lime, juiced (3 tbsp)

⅓ cup apple cider vinegar

¼ cup water

1 tbsp kosher salt

Spiced Ketchup

There is a difference between spicy and spiced. This recipe is the latter. Freshly ground whole spices give this versatile ketchup a robust flavour, suitable for pairing with anything from jumbo shrimp cocktail (page 223) to grilled cheese. Tomatoes work very well under pressure, allowing the ketchup to taste like it was simmered for hours.

Grind together the cloves, allspice, star anise, fennel seeds, Szechuan peppercorns, and cumin seeds using a mortar and pestle or spice grinder. Stir in the red pepper powder, salt, mustard powder, oregano, ginger, and cinnamon and set aside.

Set the machine to sauté and add the canola oil, onion, and garlic. Sauté for 4–5 minutes or until the onions are soft and just beginning to brown.

Add the spice mix and stir well to combine. Cook for 30 seconds to a minute.

Add the tomatoes, apple cider vinegar, brown sugar, and molasses, and stir well. Allow to come to a full simmer, stirring frequently to prevent scorching.

Secure the lid and set the machine for 10 minutes on high pressure. Allow for a 10-minute natural release before completely depressurizing the pot.

Remove the lid and allow to cool a little. Purée with a hand blender right in the pot.

Cool to room temperature before transferring to sealable containers or jars and refrigerating for up to 3 months.

Makes 4 cups

5 whole cloves
5 whole allspice
1 whole star anise
½ tsp fennel seeds
½ tsp Szechuan peppercorns
¼ tsp cumin seeds
2 tbsp Korean red pepper powder
1 tbsp kosher salt
1 tsp mustard powder
1 tsp dried oregano
½ tsp ground ginger
¼ tsp ground cinnamon
2 tbsp canola oil
1 medium onion, diced
5 cloves garlic
one 28-oz (796 ml) can whole plum tomatoes
½ cup apple cider vinegar
¼ cup light brown sugar
2 tbsp fancy molasses

Thai Chili Hot Sauce

Unlike many stovetop recipes where sauces tend to brown and dull during the long simmer, this one has a nice bright red colour, thanks to the electric pressure cooker's speed. Sure to become your new favourite – you'll put this sauce on everything.

Set the machine to sauté, and allow it to preheat for 4–5 minutes.

Add the peanut oil and swirl it around with a wooden spoon to coat the entire cooking surface.

Add the chilies, garlic, onions, red peppers, and coriander seeds. Don't stir! Wait about 2 minutes to allow the vegetables to take on a little colour before stirring.

Sauté for an additional 3 minutes, stirring frequently.

Stir in the tomatoes, red wine vinegar, water, salt, and fish sauce and secure the lid.

Set the machine for 10 minutes on high pressure. Once the pressure cooking cycle has finished, depressurize completely using the quick release method.

Remove the lid and use a hand blender to purée the sauce right in the pot.

Let cool to room temperature before transferring to sealable containers or jars and refrigerating for up to 3 months.

Makes 2 cups

Note: Use white wine vinegar or apple cider vinegar if you're out of red wine vinegar.

1 tbsp peanut oil

12–24 red Thai bird chilies, stems removed

6 cloves garlic

2 medium red onions, roots removed, quartered

2 large red bell peppers, quartered, seeds and stems removed

1 tbsp coriander seeds

2 large tomatoes, quartered

½ cup red wine vinegar (see Note)

½ cup water

2 tsp kosher salt

2 tsp fish sauce

Pineapple Scotch Bonnet Hot Sauce

The warmth of the Scotch bonnet is a perfect match for the tropical sweetness of the pineapple. The short pressure cooking cycle preserves the flavours, resulting in a bright, beautiful, and bodacious condiment that works well on tacos, barbecued pork, and maybe even pizza.

Place all the ingredients into the pot and secure the lid.

Set the machine for 15 minutes on high pressure. Allow for a 10-minute natural release before completely depressurizing the pot.

Remove the lid and allow the sauce to cool for a few minutes. Use a hand blender to easily purée the sauce right in the pot.

Cool to room temperature before transferring to sealable containers or jars and refrigerating for up to 3 months.

Makes about 6 cups

Notes: If you like your sauces spicy beyond reason or convention, leave the seeds in the Scotch bonnets.

This recipe is easily halved.

1 medium or large pineapple, peeled, cored, and roughly cut into 1– or 2-inch cubes

1 large Vidalia or other sweet onion, diced

2 tbsp chopped fresh ginger

1 lemon, juiced (about ¼ cup)

½ cup white wine vinegar

2 tsp kosher salt

4 Scotch bonnet peppers, halved, seeds removed (see Note)

2 sprigs fresh thyme, leaves picked off, stems discarded

Marinated Beets

Tabbouleh

Bulgur, a wheat kernel high in fibre, cooks quickly because it has been steamed before drying and cracking. Tabbouleh can be a great fresh snack or served as a side to grilled or roasted meats.

Rinse and drain the bulgur wheat and add it to the pot with the water, 1 tsp of salt, and 1 tsp of olive oil. Secure the lid.

Set the machine for 2 minutes on high pressure. Allow for a 5-minute natural release before completely depressurizing the pot.

Remove the lid and give the bulgur a little stir. Allow the bulgur to cool for 5–10 minutes before making the salad.

Place the bulgur into a large bowl. Add the red onion, tomatoes, 2 tbsp of olive oil, red wine vinegar, lemon juice, parsley, mint, and basil. Season with ½ tsp of salt and freshly ground black pepper to taste.

Mix it all together until everything is evenly coated in the dressing, and serve.

Makes 3 cups

Note: You can store undressed cooked bulgur in the fridge for up to a week to use casually in salads.

½ cup bulgur wheat (see Note)

1 cup water

1 tsp kosher salt

1 tsp olive oil

1 small red onion, finely diced

2 plum tomatoes, quartered, seeds removed, diced

2 tbsp olive oil

1 tbsp red wine vinegar

1 lemon, juiced (about ¼ cup)

½ cup chopped fresh parsley

¼ cup chopped fresh mint

¼ cup chopped fresh basil

½ tsp kosher salt

freshly ground black pepper

Marinated Beets

Beets are high in fibre and a good source of vitamins. They can be eaten when they're young and small or fully grown, and they're available all year long in many regions. Pressure cooking instead of boiling or roasting them will really change the way you look at beets because of the intense flavours.

Place the beets in the pot and add the 2 cups of water, 1 tsp of salt, and caraway seeds. Secure the lid.

Set the machine for 15 minutes on high pressure. Allow for a 10-minute natural release before completely depressurizing the pot.

Remove the beets from the water and allow to cool for 10 minutes or until you're able to handle them without burning yourself. Discard the cooking liquid.

Peel the beets and cut them into wedges – fours or sixes, depending on the size of the beet – and transfer them to a bowl.

In a small bowl, whisk together the ½ cup of water, apple cider vinegar, 2 tbsp of salt, and sugar. Pour over the beets and toss to coat evenly.

Let cool to room temperature before tranferring to sealable containers or jars and refrigerating for up to a month.

Makes about 6 cups

Notes: To avoid pink hands, wear rubber gloves when you peel the beets. (They'll also act as a heat barrier.) If you don't have gloves, you can wash your hands with an egg white and the stain will rinse away.

If you want to go fancy, this recipe also works with yellow or candy cane beets.

2½ lb (16 small or medium) beets (see Notes)
2 cups water
1 tsp kosher salt
1 tsp caraway seeds
½ cup water
½ cup apple cider vinegar
2 tbsp kosher salt
2 tsp sugar

Beet Salad with Arugula and Goat Cheese

The earthy beet flavour and the tang of the tarragon, smoothed out with the creaminess of the goat cheese, are what make this recipe work. If goat cheese isn't your style, consider gorgonzola, feta, or brie as a substitute. This recipe offers just one example of the many ways you can use the marinated beets you made (page 41).

In a small bowl, mix together the shallots, apple cider vinegar, tarragon, chives, olive oil, and saba. Season with salt and freshly ground black pepper to taste.

Arrange the arugula on a platter and top with beets and goat cheese. Drizzle the shallot dressing evenly over the top, crack on some fresh pepper, and enjoy the salad right away.

Serves 4 as a meal or 8 as a side dish

Note: Saba is made from pressed grapes still in contact with their skins and seeds (grape must). Must is generally fermented and used in the wine-making process, but for saba it is slow-cooked and reduced to a sweet syrup reminiscent of an aged balsamic vinegar. It's a powerful ingredient that offers a lot of flavour. As an alternative, you can use a fine aged balsamic vinegar or pure maple or agave syrup.

2 medium shallots, thinly sliced in rings

3 tbsp apple cider vinegar

3 tbsp torn or roughly chopped fresh tarragon leaves

2 tbsp roughly chopped fresh chives

2 tbsp olive oil

1 tbsp saba (see Note)

½ tsp kosher salt

freshly ground black pepper

6 cups arugula

3 cups marinated beets (page 41)

4 oz goat cheese

Wild Rice Waldorf Salad

This recipe is based on the salad that delighted guests at the fabled Waldorf Astoria Hotel in New York City. We take it a step further. With the addition of wild rice, it's better than ever. The texture and flavour of the wild rice make it perfect as an addition to this classic salad while adding a little protein into the mix.

Place the rice, water, and ¼ tsp of salt into the pot and secure the lid.

Set the machine for 15 minutes on high pressure, allowing or a 10-minute natural release before completely depressurizing the pot.

Transfer the cooked wild rice to a bowl and allow to cool to room temperature before adding the apples, celery root, grapes, lemon juice, mayonnaise, sour cream, 1 tsp of salt, and freshly ground black pepper.

Toss to coat and serve garnished with the chopped walnuts.

Serves 4–6

1 cup wild rice, rinsed and
   drained
1½ cups water
¼ tsp kosher salt
2 Granny Smith apples, cut
   into ½-inch dice
2 cups julienned celery root
1½ cups green seedless
   grapes, halved
1 lemon, juiced (about ¼ cup)
½ cup mayonnaise
¼ cup sour cream
1 tsp kosher salt
freshly ground black pepper
½ cup chopped walnuts

One-Pot Quinoa Power Bowl

Quinoa is a seed, not a grain, and is considered a whole protein because of its abundance of essential amino acids. It's easy to cook and complements many other foods, like this power salad. If you want to make more quinoa than the recipe calls for, keep the quinoa and water at a 1:1 ratio.

Rinse and drain the quinoa. Add the quinoa to the pot with the ⅔ cup of water and the ½ tsp of salt.

Place the trivet in the pot and set the 2 eggs on it.

Secure the lid and set the machine for 1 minute on high pressure. Allow for a 10-minute natural release before completely depressurizing the pot. The pressure indicator may say it's completely depressurized before the 10 minutes are up, but allow for a full 10 minutes before opening the lid.

Remove the lid and take out the eggs and the trivet. Place the eggs into a bowl of cold water for 3–4 minutes before peeling. Then give the quinoa a little stir. Allow it to cool 5–10 minutes before turning it into salad.

For the dressing, in a small bowl, whisk together the ¼ cup of water, olive oil, tahini, honey, 1 tsp of salt, and lime juice. Season with freshly ground black pepper and set aside.

Cut each peeled egg into halves or quarters.

Divide the quinoa into bowls, top with the eggs and vegetable garnishes, and drizzle with the tahini dressing.

Serves 4

Note: This recipe is easily doubled.

⅔ cup quinoa

⅔ cup water

½ tsp kosher salt

2 large eggs

For the dressing:

¼ cup water

¼ cup olive oil

2 tbsp tahini

2 tsp liquid honey

1 tsp kosher salt

1 lime, juiced (3 tbsp)

freshly ground black pepper

Suggested garnishes:

1 cup cherry tomatoes, halved

½ cucumber, sliced or diced

1 large carrot, grated, sliced, or peeled in strips

1–2 avocados, sliced or diced

2 cups salad greens and/or sprouts

Village-Style Chickpea Greek Salad

Chickpeas from the pressure cooker will be among your favourite things once you try this recipe. The chickpeas cook up perfectly tender, with a creamy centre. The skins remain intact and provide a little texture for the tooth.

Place the dried chickpeas into a container large enough to hold double the volume. Cover with at least twice the amount of water and refrigerate for a minimum of 12 hours, although 24 hours is ideal.

Drain and rinse the soaked chickpeas and add them to the pot with the 2 cups of water, 2 tsp of salt, and 1 tbsp of olive oil and secure the lid.

Set the machine for 20 minutes on high pressure. Allow for a 10-minute natural release before completely depressurizing the pot.

Remove the lid and strain the chickpeas, discarding the cooking liquid. Allow the chickpeas to cool to room temperature before preparing the rest of the salad.

Place the cooled chickpeas into a large bowl. Add the red onion, red pepper, cucumber, tomatoes, olives, red wine vinegar, 3 tbsp of olive oil, oregano, garlic, lemon juice, and 2 tsp of salt, and season to taste with freshly ground black pepper. Use a pair of large spoons to mix it all together until everything is evenly coated in the dressing. Top the salad with feta cheese and serve.

Makes 8 cups

Note: This salad can marinate for up to 24 hours.

1 cup dried chickpeas

2 cups water

2 tsp kosher salt

1 tbsp olive oil

1 medium red onion, sliced

1 red bell pepper, diced

1 cucumber, diced

1 pint grape or cherry
   tomatoes, halved

1 cup kalamata (black) olives,
   pits or no pits (chef's choice)

¼ cup red wine vinegar

3 tbsp olive oil

2 tbsp chopped fresh oregano

1 large clove garlic, minced

½ lemon, juiced (2 tbsp)

2 tsp kosher salt

freshly ground black pepper

½ lb feta cheese, cubed or
   crumbled

Bavarian Potato Salad

This southern German staple, ubiquitous alongside any size or variety of wurst, is served in most every gasthaus with a view of the Alps. It's the creamiest potato salad ever, yet dairy free. Strap on your lederhosen and give it a try. A salad and a side dish in one.

Add the potatoes, chicken stock, and salt to the pot and secure the lid.

Set the machine for 5 minutes on high pressure. Allow for a 5-minute natural release before completely depressurizing the pot.

Remove the lid and fold in the canola oil, apple cider vinegar, and freshly ground black pepper, stirring to combine and break up some of the potatoes until you get a creamy consistency. Don't worry if it looks soupy. Once the salad cools down, it thickens up on its own. Cool to room temperature before adding the green onions and serving.

Serves 4

2 lb Yukon gold potatoes
   (about 6 medium), peeled
   and cut into 1-inch dice
1¼ cups chicken stock
2 tsp kosher salt
5 tbsp canola oil
¼ cup apple cider vinegar
freshly ground black pepper
3 green onions, finely sliced

Israeli Couscous, Tomato, and Bocconcini Salad

Israeli couscous, invented in the 1950s as a substitute for rice, is a rather new entry in the food history books. It's much larger than regular couscous, and part of its production process involves toasting the pearls to dry them – resulting in a nuttier flavour than that of its little cousin. There's a good amount of olive oil in this recipe, and fresh bread is a must for sopping up the extra vinaigrette.

Set the machine to sauté.

Put the couscous into the pot with 1 tbsp of olive oil. Sauté for 4–6 minutes to lightly brown.

Add the water and ½ tsp salt and stir.

Secure the lid and set the machine for 1 minute on high pressure. Allow for a 5-minute natural release before completely depressurizing the pot.

Remove the lid and stir in 1 tbsp of olive oil. Transfer the couscous to a large bowl. Once the couscous is cool, you're ready to make the salad.

To the bowl with the couscous, add the tomatoes, bocconcini, basil, balsamic vinegar, ¼ cup of olive oil, 2 tsp salt, and freshly ground black pepper.

Toss everything together and serve.

Makes about 6 cups

Note: Israeli couscous cooked in chicken stock and butter makes a great warm side dish on its own.

1 cup Israeli couscous
   (see Note)
1 tbsp olive oil
1 cup water
½ tsp kosher salt
1 tbsp olive oil
2 cups cherry or grape
   tomatoes, halved
1 cup baby bocconcini, each
   ball sliced in thirds
1 cup fresh basil leaves,
   roughly chopped
¼ cup balsamic vinegar
¼ cup olive oil
2 tsp kosher salt
freshly ground black pepper

Three-Bean Summer Succotash Salad

If you have corn and lima beans, you have a succotash waiting to happen. This can be one of those clean-out-the-vegetable-drawer salads, where anything goes. Throw in tomatoes, switch up the romano beans for whatever you have, toss in arugula or spinach right before serving. This make-ahead salad, packed with vitamins and nutrients, is perfect for the crowd at your next family gathering, potluck, or barbecue.

Place the dried beans into a container large enough to hold double the volume. Cover with 4 cups of water and refrigerate for a minimum of 12 hours, although 24 hours is ideal.

Drain and rinse the soaked beans and add them to the pot with the 2 cups of water, 1 tsp of salt, and 1 tbsp of olive oil. Secure the lid.

Set the machine for 15 minutes on high pressure. Allow for a 10-minute natural release before completely depressurizing the pot.

Remove the lid and strain the beans, discarding the cooking liquid. Allow them to cool to room temperature before making the rest of the salad.

Place the cooled beans into a large bowl. Add the green beans, red pepper, red onion, corn, herbs, red wine vinegar, ¼ cup of olive oil, garlic, sugar, and 1 tbsp of salt, and season to taste with freshly ground black pepper. Use a pair of large spoons to mix it all together until everything is evenly coated in the dressing. Cover, refrigerate, and allow to marinate for a minimum of 1 hour, though overnight is best.

Makes 10 cups

Notes: If you're using frozen corn, thaw and drain the excess water before adding the kernels to the recipe. If using fresh, see photo on page 111 for preparation tip.

This recipe is easily halved.

1 cup dried romano beans

1 cup dried lima beans

2 cups water

1 tsp kosher salt

1 tbsp olive oil

4 cups green beans, sliced on the bias, into ¼-inch pieces

1 red bell pepper, thinly sliced into 1-inch pieces

1 medium red onion, thinly sliced

1 cup corn kernels (see Note)

1 cup chopped fresh herbs (such as parsley, oregano, and chives)

¾ cup red wine vinegar

¼ cup olive oil

2 cloves garlic, minced

1 tbsp sugar

1 tbsp kosher salt

freshly ground black pepper

Vegetable Stock

VEGETABLES
AND SIDES

Red Wine and Apple–Braised Red Cabbage

Next time you find yourself looking for side dishes for a roast, give this one a try. It's tangy and sweet, and it goes great with gravy. With traditional braising methods, this recipe can take the better part of an hour to cook as the cabbage breaks down slowly while you stir it constantly. In this recipe, the pressure inside the machine works on every surface of the shredded cabbage. So the vegetable cooks in extremely short order. It also holds up well, so you can keep it warm while you finish preparing the rest of your meal.

In a large bowl, mix together all the ingredients and allow to sit 20–30 minutes, tossing at least once during that time.

Add everything to the pot and secure the lid.

Set the machine for 5 minutes on high pressure, allowing for a 5-minute natural release before depressurizing completely.

Remove the lid and serve.

Serves 4–6

½ head red cabbage, thinly sliced (about 6 cups)

1 medium red onion, thinly sliced

1 apple, peeled and thinly sliced

3 tsp kosher salt

½ cup cranberries, fresh or frozen

½ cup red wine

¼ cup apple cider vinegar or red wine vinegar

2 tbsp butter

2 tbsp pure maple syrup

¼ tsp ground cinnamon

¼ tsp ground cloves

Vegetable Stock

Using vegetable stock in place of water in soups and stews adds an extra layer of goodness with very little extra cost. The stock is traditionally simmered for at least an hour, but your pressure cooker will have it ready in half the time – and without steaming up your kitchen.

Place all the ingredients into the pot and secure the lid.

Set the machine for 15 minutes on high pressure.

Once the pressure cooking cycle has finished, allow for a full natural release.

Remove the lid and allow to cool 5–10 minutes before straining. Discard the spent vegetable matter and keep the glorious broth, refrigerated, for 2 weeks, or freeze for up to 3 months.

Makes 12 cups

Note: Waste not, want not. Save vegetable scraps such as onion peels, herb stems, and carrot and celery tops and bottoms. Freeze them and make this stock when you've accumulated enough.

2½ lb vegetables – carrots, tomatoes, onions, celery, mushroom stems, leeks; any combination is fine, but avoid eggplant

about 1 cup fresh parsley and other herbs (including leaves and stems); any combination is fine, but avoid rosemary

2 bay leaves

1 slice dried porcini mushroom

1 tbsp miso paste

3 quarts cold water

1 tsp kosher salt

1 tsp black peppercorns

Tomato Sauce

It's real simple. The electric pressure cooker does a wonderful job creating robust tomato flavours in a short time. The high temperature inside the pot allows the tomatoes to go through the Maillard reaction, resulting in a sumptuous, full-flavoured sauce. You can double this recipe and pack it away in the freezer, ready for when you need it.

Set the machine to sauté and add the olive oil, onion, garlic, and salt. Sauté for 3–4 minutes to soften.

Add the tomatoes and basil, season with freshly ground black pepper, and stir well to break up the tomatoes a little.

Secure the lid and set the machine for 15 minutes on high pressure, allowing for a 15-minute natural release before completely depressurizing the pot.

Remove the lid.

Use a hand blender to purée the sauce right in the pot.

Makes 4 cups

¼ cup olive oil

1 large onion, roughly chopped

4 cloves garlic, roughly chopped

1 tsp kosher salt

one 28-oz (796 ml) can whole tomatoes

½ cup fresh basil

freshly ground black pepper

Chana Masala

Chickpeas are a staple of Indian cuisine and we're happy to welcome them to North America, especially when cooked in rich curry sauces like this one. In fact, chickpeas are now so popular in the Western hemisphere that North American countries round out the top 10 global producers of the pulse.

Place the dried chickpeas into a container large enough to hold double the volume. Cover with 2 cups of water and refrigerate for a minimum of 12 hours, although 24 hours is ideal.

Grind together the coriander and cumin seeds using a mortar and pestle or spice grinder. Add the garam masala, turmeric, and methi powder and set aside.

Set the machine to sauté and add the ghee, onion, garlic, ginger, and salt and sauté for 8–10 minutes, stirring frequently until fully cooked and golden brown.

Stir in the spice mix followed by the lemon juice to cool down the pot.

Drain, rinse, and add the soaked chickpeas, the 1½ cups of water, and the passata. Stir well.

Secure the lid and set the machine for 20 minutes on high pressure. Allow for a 10-minute natural release before completely depressurizing the pot.

Remove the lid, stir, and serve garnished with cilantro and Thai bird chili if desired.

Makes 4 cups

1 cup dried chickpeas

1 tbsp coriander seeds

1 tsp cumin seeds

1 tsp garam masala

1 tsp turmeric

1 tsp methi (fenugreek) powder (optional, but delicious)

2 tbsp ghee

1 medium onion, finely diced

3 large cloves garlic, chopped

2 tbsp chopped fresh ginger

2 tsp kosher salt

1 lemon, juiced (about ¼ cup)

1½ cups water

1 cup passata

chopped fresh cilantro (optional)

1 red Thai bird chili, stem and seeds removed, chopped or sliced (optional)

Dal Makhani

This popular dish is traditionally reserved for special occasions because of its long, drawn-out preparation. Good news! The electric pressure cooker will speed things up tremendously and have you enjoying it any time you're in the mood. Its deep, rich flavour and creamy butter and yogurt finish make this dish special. It can be served on its own or as a side to grilled chicken or pork chops. Feature it alongside aloo gobi (page 85) and chana masala (page 63) for your own Indian buffet at home.

Place the kidney beans into a container large enough to hold double the volume. Cover with 1 cup of water and refrigerate for a minimum of 12 hours, although 24 hours is ideal.

Grind together the cardamom pods, cumin seeds, cloves, and cinnamon using a mortar and pestle or spice grinder. Pass through a not-too-fine sieve to remove the cardamom pod skins and any large cinnamon pieces. Set aside.

Set the machine to sauté and add the ghee, shallots, garlic, ginger, serrano pepper, and salt. Sauté, stirring frequently, for 4–5 minutes or until the mixture is lightly browned.

Add the spice mix and stir well to incorporate it, followed by the lime juice to cool down the pot.

Add the 3 cups of water or chicken stock, passata, black lentils, and soaked, drained, and rinsed kidney beans.

Stir well and secure the lid.

Set the machine for 15 minutes on high pressure. Allow for a 15-minute natural release before completely depressurizing the pot.

Remove the lid, stir in the butter, and serve with the yogurt and fresh cilantro.

Makes 6 cups

½ cup dried kidney beans

8 cardamom pods

3 tsp cumin seeds

3 whole cloves

1-inch piece cinnamon stick

2 tbsp ghee

3 shallots, finely diced

3 cloves garlic, minced

1 tbsp minced fresh ginger

1 serrano pepper, minced

1 tsp kosher salt

½ lime, juiced (1½ tbsp)

3 cups water or chicken stock

2 cups passata

1½ cups dried black lentils, rinsed and drained

2 tbsp butter

plain full-fat yogurt

chopped fresh cilantro

Cuban Black Beans

A sofrito of onions and peppers is used to liven up the black beans, which can be rich and heavy at times. Sofritos come in many varieties from around the world, but they share a purpose: to add subtle flavour builders and, in this recipe, a little crunch. This side dish goes remarkably well with barbecued pork ribs and chicken.

Place the dried black beans into a container large enough to hold double the volume. Cover with 4 cups of water and refrigerate for a minimum of 12 hours, although 24 hours is ideal.

Set the machine to sauté and add the ghee, celery, red onions, poblano peppers, garlic, bay leaf, thyme, cumin seeds, and salt. Sauté, stirring frequently until the vegetables are soft and starting to brown, about 7–8 minutes.

Add the soaked, drained, and rinsed black beans, followed by the chicken stock, and stir well.

Secure the lid and set the machine for 10 minutes on high pressure. Allow for an 8-minute natural release before completely depressurizing the pot.

For the sofrito, in a bowl, mix together the reserved red onions and poblano peppers with the red pepper, agave syrup, apple cider vinegar, hot sauce, dark rum, and chopped cilantro.

Remove the lid, stir in the sofrito, and serve.

Makes 4 cups

Note: Lime juice can be substituted for the apple cider vinegar.

2 cups dried black beans

2 tbsp ghee

1 stalk celery, finely diced

2 medium red onions, finely diced (reserve 25% for the sofrito)

2 poblano peppers, finely diced (reserve 25% for the sofrito)

5 cloves garlic, minced

1 bay leaf

2 tbsp chopped fresh thyme

1 tsp cumin seeds

2 tsp kosher salt

2 cups chicken stock

½ red bell pepper, finely diced

1 tbsp agave syrup

2 tbsp apple cider vinegar (see Note)

1 tbsp hot sauce

½ oz dark rum

½ cup chopped fresh cilantro

Collard Greens with Sausage and Peppers

Collard greens are popular in the South, often prepared with smoked or salted meats such as bacon. It's a hardy green – a relative of cabbage and broccoli and one of the best natural sources of Vitamin K, right up there with kale and spinach. This recipe begs to be served with rice or bread – cornbread is ideal – for sopping up the nutrient-rich pot liquor.

Set the machine to sauté and allow it to preheat for 4–5 minutes.

Add 1 tbsp butter to the pot and allow it to heat up for a few seconds. Place the sausage meat into the pot, dispersing it evenly in the bottom. However tempting, don't stir up the meat for about 5 minutes. This will allow the meat to caramelize to a nice golden brown on one side.

Stir it all up and add the onions, red and yellow peppers, garlic, and salt, and season to taste with freshly ground black pepper. Sauté, stirring frequently, for 2 minutes.

Stir in the wine, and then add the collards to the pot without stirring them.

Secure the lid and set the machine for 12 minutes on high pressure. Once the pressure cooking cycle has finished, depressurize completely using the quick release method.

Remove the lid and transfer the sausage and the vegetables to a plate or bowl, leaving the juices in the pot.

Set the machine to sauté and simmer the sauce for 4–5 minutes to reduce the liquid and thicken it up a bit.

Turn off the machine when the desired consistency is reached and stir in the remaining 2 tbsp butter.

Pour the sauce over the sausage and collards and serve.

Serves 4

1 tbsp butter

4 hot Italian sausages (approximately 1 lb) – (feel free to substitute your preference – chef's choice), casings removed

2 medium onions, sliced into ½-inch strips

1 red bell pepper, sliced into ½-inch strips

1 yellow pepper, sliced into ½-inch strips

2 cloves garlic, sliced

1 tsp kosher salt

freshly ground black pepper

¼ cup white wine

1 bunch (about 8 cups chopped) collard greens, largest stems removed, sliced into 1-inch strips

2 tbsp butter

Honey-Glazed Carrots

These carrots taste like . . . carrots – big, deliciously sweet, zesty carrots. The pressure cooker's uncanny ability to intensify flavours is particularly evident in this simple preparation. The carrots are perfectly cooked, and all the flavour stays within them (see photo on page 58).

Set the machine to sauté and add the carrots, ginger, butter, and salt, and season to taste with freshly ground black pepper. Sauté for 2–3 minutes, stirring frequently to get things rolling.

Add the honey and the chicken stock, stir once, and secure the lid.

Set the machine for 3 minutes on high pressure. Once the pressure cooking cycle has finished, depressurize completely using the quick release method.

Remove the lid and serve.

Serves 4–6 as a side dish

Note: Add a layer of flavour by using really good honey. Check your farmers' market for a local producer.

1½ lb carrots, peeled and
   sliced on a bias, ¼-inch thick
   (about 5 cups)
½ tsp minced fresh ginger
1 tbsp butter
1 tsp kosher salt
freshly ground black pepper
¼ cup honey (see Note)
2 tbsp chicken stock (or water)

Farro with Tomatoes and Swiss Chard

Farro is a happy little wheat grain similar to spelt or wheat berries, and it can be a tasty substitute for rice or barley. This recipe, prepared simply with fresh tomatoes and Swiss chard, is cooked to the perfect consistency in the electric pressure cooker. It's tender with a slight bite and never mushy.

Set the machine to sauté and add the olive oil, onion, garlic, salt, chili flakes, and ground fennel. Sauté, stirring frequently, for 4–5 minutes.

Add the farro and continue to cook for 1 minute.

Add the white wine, followed by the water and the tomatoes.

Secure the lid and set the machine for 10 minutes on high pressure. Once the pressure cooking cycle has finished, depressurize completely using the quick release method.

Remove the lid and set the machine to sauté. Stir in the Swiss chard and cook, stirring, for about 2 minutes. Turn the machine off.

Stir in the Parmesan cheese and the fresh herbs and serve.

Makes 4 cups

2 tbsp olive oil

1 small onion, finely diced

2 cloves garlic, minced

2 tsp kosher salt

½ tsp chili flakes

½ tsp fennel seeds, freshly ground in a mortar and pestle or spice grinder

1 cup farro, rinsed and drained

¼ cup white wine

2 cups water

1 pint cherry or grape tomatoes, halved

2 cups thinly sliced Swiss chard

½ cup grated Parmesan cheese

½ cup chopped fresh herbs (such as parsley, basil, and chives)

Creamy Brussels Sprouts with Pancetta

Admittedly, brussels sprouts don't have a delicious reputation, but that's about to change in your house. With salty pancetta combined with the creamy finish, even your kids will be asking for more. A great side dish for fall and winter meals, and it will fit right in at Thanksgiving dinner.

Set the machine to sauté and add the butter and pancetta. Sauté for 3–4 minutes.

Add the onion, salt, and nutmeg, and season to taste with freshly ground black pepper. Sauté for 3–4 minutes until the onion is soft and just starting to brown.

Add the white wine and cook for 30 seconds.

Place the brussels sprouts in the pot (don't bother to stir them in) and secure the lid.

Set the machine for 4 minutes on high pressure. Once the pressure cooking cycle has finished, depressurize completely using the quick release method.

Remove the lid and set the machine to sauté. Stir in the cream and bring to a simmer for 1 minute.

Turn off the machine and wait a few minutes before serving.

Serves 6–8

Note: Regular or double-smoked bacon can be substituted for the pancetta.

1 tbsp butter

½ cup pancetta, cut into lardons (see Note)

1 small onion, finely diced

1 tsp kosher salt

pinch nutmeg (preferably freshly grated)

freshly ground black pepper

¼ cup white wine

4 cups brussels sprouts, halved through the stems

⅔ cup 35% cream

Buttered Spaghetti Squash

Finally! A spaghetti squash recipe that doesn't include spaghetti sauce. The flavour intensifies under pressure, and all you need are a few simple ingredients to enhance it even further. Serve this member of the cucurbit family anytime, especially if there's a roasted turkey involved.

Add the wine to the pot. Evenly arrange the squash in the pot, add the salt, and secure the lid.

Set the machine for 7 minutes on high pressure. Once the pressure cooking cycle has finished, depressurize completely using the quick release method.

Remove the lid and add the butter, parsley, and green onions, and season to taste with freshly ground black pepper.

Stir the ingredients to break up the squash and combine the butter and herbs. Serve immediately.

Serves 4–6

¼ cup white wine

1 spaghetti squash, peeled, seeds removed, and cut into 8 chunks (see Note)

2 tsp kosher salt

¼ cup butter, cubed

¼ cup chopped fresh parsley

2 green onions, finely sliced

freshly ground black pepper

Note: Cut the squash along the grain for longer shreds and against the grain for shorter ones.

Greek Lemon Potatoes

Teeming with lemon and garlic flavours, these potatoes are great to serve beside your skewers or grilled chops.

Place all the ingredients into a resealable bag or container and marinate, refrigerated, for 2–4 hours or overnight.

Arrange the potatoes cut side down, as best you can, in the pot and pour in the marinade.

Secure the lid and set the machine for 8 minutes on high pressure. Once the pressure cooking cycle has finished, depressurize completely using the quick release method.

Remove the lid and serve.

Serves 4–6

2 lb Yukon gold potatoes (about 6 medium), peeled and halved
3 cloves garlic, minced
¾ cup chicken stock
1 lemon, juiced (about ¼ cup)
3 tbsp olive oil
1 tbsp chopped fresh oregano
2 tsp kosher salt
freshly ground black pepper to taste

Red Wine Balsamic Mushrooms

Enjoy marinated mushrooms just like the ones you get on an antipasto platter at that little Italian place in town (pictured with eggplant caponata on page 78). Serve chilled on charcuterie boards or cheese platters, or eat them one at a time, straight out of the jar. The electric pressure cooker does a great job cooking mushrooms so that they're not dried out or chewy.

In a large bowl, stir together the red wine, balsamic vinegar, rosemary, and salt, and season to taste with freshly ground black pepper.

Add the mushrooms and toss well to coat evenly. Marinate for 5–10 minutes to soften the mushrooms and allow them to begin releasing water.

Add everything to the pot and secure the lid.

Set the machine for 5 minutes on high pressure. Once the pressure cooking cycle has finished, depressurize completely using the quick release method.

Remove the lid and set the machine to sauté. Cook for 5–7 minutes to boil off some of the liquid or until the desired consistency is reached.

Turn the machine off and allow mushrooms to cool to room temperature – unless you prefer to eat them hot. (See Note.) Transfer the cooled mushrooms to a sealable container or jar and refrigerate for up to 2 weeks.

Makes 2 cups

Notes: Cut extra-large mushrooms in half or quarters.

You can also eat the mushrooms while they're hot. Add a tablespoon of butter once you've turned off the machine and serve as a laid-back side dish for steaks or chops, or on a simple leafy green salad.

¼ cup red wine

1 tbsp balsamic vinegar

1 tsp chopped fresh rosemary

1 tsp kosher salt

freshly ground black pepper

1 lb small button mushrooms, washed and patted dry (see Note)

Eggplant Caponata

This antipasto classic with a zillion versions is nice to have on hand whether you need to throw together a last-minute cheese plate for guests or are looking to spruce up your pizza. This version is close to the style made in Sicily and is best served at room temperature.

Place the eggplant in a bowl and season evenly with the salt. Set aside for 1 hour to allow the eggplant to cure and release a little water. Rinse the eggplant in water and pat dry.

Set the pot to sauté and add the olive oil, onion, celery, and serrano pepper. Cook, stirring frequently, for 5–6 minutes or until the vegetables are softened and almost starting to brown.

Add the eggplant, olives, capers, anchovies, tomatoes, pine nuts, and white wine vinegar, and stir well to combine.

Secure the lid and set the machine for 3 minutes on high pressure. Once the pressure cooking cycle has finished, depressurize completely using the quick release method.

Remove the lid. Give the caponata one nice stir, but avoid breaking up the eggplant too much.

Cool, uncovered, to allow for evaporation before packing up and refrigerating (see Note).

It will keep for up to a month, tightly sealed and refrigerated.

Makes 6 cups

Note: Once the caponata has cooled, pack it into wide-mouth jars for easy fridge-to-table action.

1 medium eggplant, skin on, quartered lengthwise and sliced into ½-inch pieces

1 tbsp kosher salt

⅓ cup olive oil

1 large sweet onion, diced

1 stalk celery, diced

1 serrano pepper, thinly sliced in rings

½ cup green olives, pitted and roughly chopped

1 tbsp capers, roughly chopped

4 anchovy filets, roughly chopped

3 medium plum tomatoes, quartered lengthwise, seeds removed, cut into ½-inch dice

¼ cup pine nuts

1 tbsp white wine vinegar

Garlic Confit

If you have an aversion to chopping or mincing garlic, this recipe is for you. Keep garlic confit in the fridge and add clove-sized spoonfuls at will. No chopping required. This pot-in-pot recipe gives you a strong yet smooth flavour enhancer for soups, stews, dressings, and marinades. It takes only a minute to prepare for the machine and won't have your oven running for hours. You'll need the trivet for the bottom of the pot, a 6-inch round cake pan (3 inches deep), and some aluminum foil.

Place the garlic, olive oil, and salt in a 6-inch round cake pan and stir together. Cover the pan with foil, crimping the edges to form a tight seal.

Pour the cup of water into the bottom of the pot and place the trivet inside. Place the pan onto the trivet.

Secure the lid and set the machine for 45 minutes on high pressure. Once the pressure cycle has finished, depressurize completely using the quick release method.

Remove the lid and wait about 10 minutes for everything to cool down before carefully removing the pan from the machine.

Mash up the garlic with a fork or potato masher, or leave the cloves whole and mash them up as needed.

Transfer the garlic to a sealable container or jar and refrigerate. Will keep for up to 2 months.

Makes 1 cup

Note: Speed up the process by purchasing peeled garlic, available in many grocery stores.

36 cloves peeled garlic (about 1 cup) (see Note)
⅓ cup olive oil
1 tsp kosher salt
1 cup water, for steaming

Potato and Leek Champ

Champ, a simple offering coming to us from Ireland, originally contained just potato and onion. Here is a slightly elevated version with the addition of leeks and buttermilk (see photo on page 58). The buttermilk offers its signature tang to the dish.

Add the potatoes, leeks, the water, butter, and salt to the pot, and secure the lid.

Set the machine for 8 minutes on high pressure.

Once the pressure cooking cycle has finished, turn off the machine and depressurize completely using the quick release method.

Remove the lid, add the buttermilk and nutmeg, and season to taste with freshly ground black pepper.

Use a sturdy whisk or potato masher to mash the potatoes until they've absorbed all the buttermilk. Mash to the desired texture – lumpy or smooth.

Serve immediately beside steak, chops, ribs, or anything else of your choosing.

Makes 6 cups

Note: Tuck the dark green part of the leek into the freezer for the next time you make stock.

2½ lb Yukon gold potatoes (about 7 medium), peeled, cut into 1-inch chunks
2 leeks, white and light green sections only, halved lengthwise, washed well, and cut into 1-inch pieces (see Note)
⅓ cup water
¼ cup butter
2 tsp kosher salt
⅓ cup buttermilk
pinch ground nutmeg
freshly ground black pepper

Roasted Garlic Mashed Potatoes

Roasted garlic is so easy to make in your electric pressure cooker, and here's one reason you should give it a try. Garlic, when roasted, has a sweet and mellow flavour that turns everyday mashed potatoes into a modern classic. Serve alongside veal osso buco (page 159), les short ribs (page 151), or beef pot roast stroganoff (page 149).

Add the potatoes, the water, and salt to the pot, and secure the lid.

Set the machine for 8 minutes on high pressure.

Once the pressure cooking cycle has finished, depressurize completely using the quick release method.

Remove the lid, add the cream, milk, butter, and garlic confit, and season to taste with freshly ground black pepper,

Use a sturdy whisk or potato masher to mash the potatoes until they've absorbed all the dairy ingredients. Mash to the desired texture – lumpy or smooth.

Serve immediately.

Makes 6 cups

3 lb Yukon gold potatoes (about 8 medium), peeled, cut into 1-inch pieces
¾ cup water
2 tsp kosher salt
½ cup 35% cream
½ cup 2% milk
¼ cup butter
3 tbsp garlic confit (page 81)
freshly ground black pepper

Aloo Gobi

Half potato, half cauliflower, all delicious. This Indian side dish is great with grilled meats and vegetables, or alongside a crisp vegetable salad. A traditional version of this recipe would have you put the potatoes and cauliflower in at different stages of the recipe because they have different cooking times. For the electric pressure cooker, the potatoes are cut small and the cauliflower is left in rather large pieces to align the cooking times and allow them to reach the proper texture simultaneously.

Set the machine to sauté and add the ghee.

Allow the ghee to melt and add the onion, serrano pepper, cumin seeds, and salt. Cook for 4–5 minutes or until the mixture starts to caramelize. Stir in the garam masala, turmeric, and tomato paste. Add 1–2 tbsp of the water to cool down the pot a little, so you don't burn the spices.

Add the rest of the water and the lime juice, followed by the potatoes and cauliflower. Give everything a good stir and secure the lid.

Set the machine to 5 minutes on high pressure. Once the pressure cooking cycle has finished, depressurize completely using the quick release method.

Remove the lid and stir the ingredients a little – but don't overdo it – to break up the cauliflower.

Serve with cilantro, lime wedges, and a spoonful of full-fat yogurt.

Makes 6 cups

Note: Serrano peppers are pretty spicy. To reduce the heat, use half a pepper. But don't remove it entirely since it lends an important nuance to the dish.

2 tbsp ghee

1 small red onion, thinly sliced

1 serrano pepper, thinly sliced in rings (see Note)

2 tsp cumin seeds

2 tsp kosher salt

1 tsp garam masala

1 tsp turmeric

1 tbsp tomato paste

1¼ cups water

½ lime, juiced (1½ tbsp)

2 large Yukon gold potatoes, cut into 1-inch dice

1 small cauliflower, broken up into 5 or 6 big pieces

fresh cilantro, lime wedges, and plain full-fat yogurt for garnishing

Potato Goulash

An Austrian dish that may rekindle the old "fork versus spoon" debate since this potato goulash recipe can be considered a soup, a stew, or a side. Closely related to the beef version (page 157), this one has the benefit of the potato starch to help bring the sauce together. The sour cream mellows out the seasonings, making this a comforting rainy day dish. Peeling the potatoes is your call – the goulash is good with the skins on or off.

Set the machine to sauté and add the butter, onions, and salt. Sauté, stirring frequently, for 15–20 minutes or until the onions are cooked and golden brown.

Add the garlic, marjoram, caraway seeds, and chili flakes, and season to taste with lots of freshly ground black pepper. Stir to incorporate.

Add the potatoes and stir in the stock.

Secure the lid and set the machine for 5 minutes on high pressure, allowing for a 5-minute natural release before completely depressurizing the pot.

Remove the lid and serve, garnished with a spoonful of sour cream and some fresh chives.

Serves 4–6

Note: Oregano is a good substitute for marjoram.

3 tbsp butter

2 large onions, thinly sliced

1 tsp kosher salt

2 cloves garlic, minced

1 tsp dried marjoram
(see Note)

¼ tsp caraway seeds

¼ tsp chili flakes

freshly ground black pepper

2 lb Yukon gold potatoes
(about 6 medium), cut into
1-inch dice

3 cups chicken, beef, or
vegetable stock

⅓ cup sour cream

chopped fresh chives
for garnishing

Salt Potatoes

Known as *salzkartoffeln* in Germany, salt potatoes are an option on most every gasthaus menu, serving to sop up the traditional saucy main dishes. Try these with Hungarian beef goulash (pictured here; recipe page 157).

Place the water and butter in the pot.

Season the potatoes with salt and add them to the pot, arranged evenly in a single layer, if possible.

Secure the lid and set the machine for 8 minutes on high pressure. Once the pressure cooking cycle has finished, depressurize completely using the quick release method.

Remove the lid, strain off the excess water, and serve.

Serves 4–6 as a side dish

Note: Garnish with chopped parsley and butter before serving and you get a whole new dish – parsley potatoes.

1 cup water

1 tbsp butter

2 lb Yukon gold potatoes (about 6 medium), peeled and halved

2 tsp kosher salt

Gai Lan with Fried Tofu in Miso Broth

Gai lan, also known as Chinese broccoli, has thick, sturdy stems and rugged leaves that allow it to stand up to the rigours of a quick pressure cooker cycle, without overcooking. Fried tofu, a firm variety that has been deep-fried before packaging, can be found in Asian markets alongside other tofu and bean curd products. With a lot more flavour than the plain variety, fried tofu works well with the distinct flavours of the miso.

Place the gai lan evenly into the bottom of the pot and place the tofu pieces on top.

In a small bowl, mix together the chili, vegetable stock, miso paste, soy sauce, garlic, ginger, sesame oil, and sesame seeds.

Pour the mixture evenly over the tofu and gai lan.

Secure the lid and set the machine for 1 minute on high pressure. Once the pressure cooking cycle has finished, depressurize completely using the quick release method.

Remove the lid and serve with rice.

Serves 4

1½ lb gai lan (Chinese broccoli), stems trimmed
10 oz fried tofu, cut into 1-inch cubes
1 red finger chili, thinly sliced in rings
⅓ cup vegetable stock
2 tbsp miso paste
2 tbsp soy sauce
1 clove garlic, minced
1 tbsp chopped fresh ginger
1 tbsp sesame oil
1 tsp sesame seeds

Macaroni and Cheese

No electric pressure cooker cookbook is complete without a recipe for macaroni and cheese. It takes about the same time as the popular boxed versions you can buy but is made with simple, real ingredients. Be prepared to make a second batch!

Add the water, onion, macaroni, butter, salt, mustard, and nutmeg to the pot and stir.

Secure the lid and set the machine for 4 minutes on high pressure. Once the pressure cooking cycle has finished, depressurize completely using the quick release method.

Remove the lid and set the machine to sauté.

Stir in the milk and cream and continue stirring while the mixture heats up, about 2 minutes.

Turn off the machine and add the cheeses, one-third at a time, stirring well each time to incorporate.

Season with freshly ground black pepper and serve.

Serves 4–6

Note: Use up odds and sods in your cheese drawer. Replace some of the Cheddar with Swiss or mozzarella cheese, or create a mix of different Cheddars from mild to old.

4 cups water

1 small onion, grated

1 lb elbow macaroni

2 tbsp butter

1 tbsp kosher salt

1 tbsp Dijon mustard

⅛ tsp freshly ground nutmeg

¾ cup 2% milk

¾ cup 35% cream

10 oz grated Cheddar cheese (see Note)

2 oz grated Parmesan cheese

freshly ground black pepper

Mushroom and Spinach Risotto

Arborio

Long-grain

Short-grain

Brown

Basmati

Parboiled

Many electric pressure cookers double as rice cookers – and they do a fine job, but why wait? Here are the basics when it comes to pressure cooking your rice quickly, consistently, and perfectly:

- Be sure to use the exact ratios of water to rice.

- Rinse rice well in cold water to eliminate loose starch (which can make the grains unnecessarily sticky), repeating until the rinse water is clear. Drain well.

- Start cooking rice immediately after rinsing or it will begin to absorb water, throwing off your ratio and cooking time.

Short-Grain Rice

Sometimes referred to as sushi rice, this sticky rice is the perfect match for gai lan with fried tofu in miso broth (page 91), or take the next step and make cucumber avocado maki (page 107).

Place the water into the pot. Add rice and salt, and stir.

Secure the lid and set the machine for 3 minutes on high pressure, allowing for a 10-minute natural release before completely depressurizing the pot.

Remove the lid, fluff the rice with a wooden spoon, and serve.

Serves 4–8

2 cups water
2 cups short-grain rice,
   rinsed and drained
½ tsp kosher salt

Long-Grain White Rice

One of the most prominent varieties, long-grain white rice is popular because of its subtle flavour and wide availability.

Place the water into the pot. Add rice, butter, and salt, and stir.

Secure the lid and set the machine for 3 minutes on high pressure, allowing for a 10-minute natural release before completely depressurizing the pot.

Remove the lid, fluff the rice with a wooden spoon, and serve.

Serves 4–8

2 cups water
2 cups long-grain white rice,
   rinsed and drained
1 tbsp butter
1½ tsp kosher salt

Basmati Rice

Basmati rice is a long and slender grain with a distinct nutty aroma. It gets its name from the Hindi word meaning "fragrant." Basmati is produced mainly in India and Pakistan and is exported all over the world. As you can imagine, basmati rice goes great with some of the Indian- and Asian-inspired dishes in this book, among them Thai green curry turkey (page 207) and butter chicken (page 193).

Place the water into the pot. Add rice and salt, and stir.

Secure the lid and set the machine for 3 minutes on high pressure, allowing for a 10-minute natural release before completely depressurizing the pot.

Remove the lid, fluff the rice with a wooden spoon, and serve.

Serves 4–8

2 cups water

2 cups basmati rice,
    rinsed and drained

1½ tsp kosher salt

Long-Grain Brown Rice

Brown rice is a whole-grain rice with only the outer hull removed, so it's a little more sturdy than white rice. Taking upward of 45 minutes to cook on the stovetop, brown rice is a perfect candidate for pressure cooking.

Place the water into the pot. Add rice, butter, and salt, and stir.

Secure the lid and set the machine for 15 minutes on high pressure, allowing for a 10-minute natural release before completely depressurizing the pot.

Remove the lid, fluff the rice with a wooden spoon, and serve.

Serves 4–8

Note: Butter helps keep the rice from sticking to the pot.

2 cups water

2 cups long-grain brown rice,
    rinsed and drained

1 tbsp butter (see Note)

1½ tsp kosher salt

Converted Rice

Converted rice is a brown rice that has been parboiled to help remove the outer husk. In the process, it drives nutrients into the grain using steam and pressure. The resulting rice has nutritional qualities closer to brown rice than to white rice. Converted rice has a tendency to cook up as single grains that don't readily stick together.

Place the water or stock into the pot. Add rice, butter, and salt, and stir.

Secure the lid and set the machine for 4 minutes on high pressure, allowing for a 10-minute natural release before completely depressurizing the pot.

Remove the lid, fluff the rice with a wooden spoon, and serve.

Serves 4–8

2¼ cups water or chicken stock

2 cups converted rice, rinsed and drained

1 tbsp butter

1½ tsp kosher salt

Wild Rice

Wild rice is actually a seed of an aquatic grass. It's harvested by hand – which speaks to its high price tag – in natural marshes in Canada (mostly in Saskatchewan and Manitoba) and the United States (Minnesota, Wisconsin, Michigan). It is longer than conventional rice and has a dark, glossy outer sheath. Wild rice goes well with fowl, whether as a side dish or in a stuffing.

Place the water into the pot. Add rice, butter, and salt, and stir.

Secure the lid and set the machine for 15 minutes on high pressure, allowing for a 10-minute natural release before completely depressurizing the pot.

Remove the lid, fluff the rice with a wooden spoon, and serve.

Serves 4–8

3 cups water

2 cups wild rice, rinsed and drained

1 tbsp butter

1½ tsp kosher salt

Mushroom and Spinach Risotto

Risotto has always been one of those dishes that chain you to your stovetop. Constant monitoring and stirring, along with the frequent addition of small amounts of liquid during the cook time, are enough to dissuade any home cook from making it. This is where the electric pressure cooker really steps up to the plate and knocks it out of the park. Discover perfect risotto, without all the stirring. Freshly grated Parmesan, decent wine, and homemade chicken stock are the keys to this one. Don't skimp on the butter, either.

Set the machine to sauté and add the 2 tbsp of butter, followed by the onion, mushrooms, and 1 tsp of salt.

Sauté, stirring frequently, for about 6 minutes or until the mushrooms just begin to brown.

Add the wine and continue to cook, stirring, until the wine has evaporated fully. Then add the chicken stock.

Stir in the arborio rice and sage, and secure the lid.

Set the machine for 6 minutes on high pressure, followed by a quick release.

Once the lid is off, immediately add the spinach, Parmesan cheese, and the other 2 tbsp of butter. Stir well for about a minute or until all the spinach has wilted and the butter and cheese are mixed in. Season to taste with salt and freshly ground black pepper.

Serve right away.

Serves 4–6

Note: If you find fresh porcini mushrooms and are willing to blow the budget, feel free to substitute them for some or all the other mushrooms. Button or cremini mushrooms can also be used.

- 2 tbsp butter
- 1 medium onion, finely diced (about the size of arborio rice grains)
- 8 oz mixed sliced mushrooms (about 3 cups) – portobello and shiitake work well (see Note)
- 1 tsp kosher salt
- ½ cup white wine
- 4 cups homemade chicken stock (page 184)
- 2 cups arborio rice
- 2 tbsp chopped fresh sage
- 4 cups lightly packed baby spinach
- ⅓ cup freshly grated Parmesan cheese
- 2 tbsp butter
- kosher salt
- freshly ground black pepper

Rice and Peas

This dish is a mainstay in the cuisines of Jamaica and other Caribbean islands, where locals refer to some beans as peas. Pigeon peas are the bean of choice, and many variations on the theme appear as you travel from island to island. Adding the fresh tomato-and-onion salsa at the end provides a dramatic fresh flavour, and it's great with jerk chicken (see photo on page 198).

Place the dried pigeon peas into a container large enough to hold double the volume. Cover with 1½ cups of water and refrigerate for a minimum of 12 hours, although 24 hours is ideal.

Set the machine to sauté and add the ghee, onion, garlic, and salt, and sauté for 5–6 minutes, stirring frequently, until fully cooked and golden brown.

Stir in the tomato paste, nutmeg, allspice, and thyme, followed closely by the chicken stock and the coconut milk.

Stir well, add the whole Scotch bonnet pepper, and bring to a simmer.

Add the rice and the soaked, drained, and rinsed pigeon peas. Stir well, and secure the lid.

Set the machine for 6 minutes on high pressure.

In a small bowl, mix together the plum tomatoes, green onions, and lime juice. Set aside.

Once the pressure cooking cycle has finished, depressurize completely using the quick release method.

Remove the lid, stir in the tomato-onion mixture, and serve.

Serves 4–6 as a side dish

¾ cup dried pigeon peas

2 tbsp ghee

1 medium onion, diced

2 cloves garlic, minced

2 tsp kosher salt

1 tbsp tomato paste

¼ tsp ground nutmeg

¼ tsp ground allspice

1 tbsp chopped fresh thyme

1½ cups chicken stock

½ cup coconut milk

1 Scotch bonnet pepper, whole

1 cup long-grain rice, rinsed and drained

2 plum tomatoes, quartered, seeds removed, and diced

2 green onions, chopped

½ lime, juiced (1½ tbsp)

Pumpkin Risotto

Not a jack-o'-lantern or pie pumpkin, but a nice Cinderella or Hokkaido variety would be the best-case scenario. Butternut squash gives nice results as well. The pumpkin seed oil garnish sets this recipe apart. It has a powerful, earthy flavour like nothing else and, for that reason, you need only a little.

Set the machine to sauté and add the 2 tbsp of butter, pumpkin, green onions, apple, thyme, leek, allspice, fennel seeds, and cinnamon. Sauté, stirring frequently, for 5–6 minutes.

Add the wine and continue to cook, stirring, until the wine has evaporated fully and then add the chicken stock.

Stir in the rice and secure the lid. Set the machine for 6 minutes on high pressure, followed by a quick release.

Remove the lid and immediately add the Parmesan cheese, parsley, and the other 2 tbsp of butter. Stir well for about a minute or until all the butter and cheese are mixed in. Season to taste with freshly ground black pepper.

Drizzle each portion with about ½ tbsp of pumpkin seed oil and serve immediately.

Serves 4–6

Note: Find pumpkin seed oil at your local specialty shops or order it online.

2 tbsp butter

4 cups pumpkin, cut into ½-inch dice

4 green onions, chopped

1 apple, cut into ½-inch dice

1 tbsp chopped fresh thyme

½ leek, white and light green sections only, halved lengthwise, washed well, and diced

½ tsp allspice, freshly ground

½ tsp fennel seeds, freshly ground

¼ tsp ground cinnamon

½ cup white wine

4 cups chicken stock

2 cups arborio rice

½ cup grated Parmesan cheese

¼ cup chopped fresh parsley

2 tbsp butter (for finishing)

freshly ground black pepper

2–3 tbsp pumpkin seed oil for garnishing (see Note)

Rice Pilaf

Rice pilaf is a somewhat lowly staple with a storied global history. The electric pressure cooker delivers it efficiently and deliciously. This recipe, simple but with its own personality, can be served alongside many great dishes. Try it with turkey breast fricassee (page 203) or beef pot roast stroganoff (page 149).

Set the machine to sauté and add the butter, onion, carrot, celery, and salt, and season to taste with freshly ground black pepper. Sauté, stirring frequently, for 4–5 minutes or until lightly softened but not yet browned.

Add the stock and bay leaf and continue to heat for 2–3 minutes.

Stir in the rice and secure the lid. Set the machine for 4 minutes on high pressure, allowing for a 10-minute natural release.

Remove the lid and serve alongside your favourite proteins – or enjoy the pilaf by itself.

Makes 5 cups

2 tbsp butter

1 small onion, finely diced

1 medium carrot, finely diced

1 stalk celery, finely diced

1 tsp kosher salt

freshly ground black pepper

2¼ cups chicken or vegetable stock

1 bay leaf

2 cups long-grain converted rice, rinsed and drained

Cucumber Avocado Maki

Making your own maki rolls may seem exotic or difficult, but it's one of the easiest recipes in this book. There's no raw fish, just the fresh crunch of the cucumber, the creamy avocado, and perfectly seasoned rice all rolled up to make an easy snack. Even the kids will get into rolling their own.

Place the rice and the water into the pot and stir.

Secure the lid and set the machine for 3 minutes on high pressure, allowing for a 10-minute natural release before completely depressurizing the pot. Remove the lid, fluff the rice with a wooden spoon, and allow to sit and steam out for 5 minutes so the rice will dry a little.

In a small bowl, mix together the rice vinegar, sugar, and salt, whisking until the solids dissolve into the liquid. Sprinkle half the vinegar mixture over the rice and gently fold it in. Repeat with the other half. You are now ready to roll your maki.

On a flat surface, place 1 sheet of nori on a thin, clean kitchen towel. Place an eighth of the rice onto the nori and spread it out flat and evenly over the bottom two-thirds of the sheet. The rice should form a rectangle about ¼–½ inch thick.

In the centre of the rice rectangle, place an eighth of the cucumber and avocado lengthwise in an elongated pile. Start the roll by bringing the closest edge of nori up and over the vegetables, tucking the nori into the rice on the other side. Finish the roll tightly so it sticks to itself. Repeat with the remaining ingredients.

Allow to rest 5 minutes before slicing. This will let the nori absorb some of the moisture from the rice, making it easier to cut.

Slice each log into about 8 rounds and serve with soy sauce, wasabi, and pickled ginger.

Makes 8 rolls

Notes: Seasoned rice vinegar has salt and sugar mixed in and can be used in place of the unseasoned variety. Just omit the salt and the sugar from this recipe.

If you make this dish a lot, invest in a nice bamboo mat for rolling.

2 cups short-grain Japanese rice (sushi rice), rinsed well and drained

2 cups water

¼ cup unseasoned rice vinegar (see Note)

2 tsp sugar

1 tsp kosher salt

8 sheets nori (seaweed sheets), about 8–9 inches square

1 cucumber, peeled and cut into 3-inch-long matchsticks

1 ripe avocado, sliced into thin strips

soy sauce

wasabi paste

pickled ginger

Cheeseburger Soup

Corn Chowder

Fresh corn on the cob is such a simple, sweet, and satisfying food. With the option of making a quick corn stock to start, this will be one of the corniest corn chowders you've ever had. Make this chowder during corn season for the best results.

To make the stock, put all the corn stock ingredients into the pot and secure the lid.

Set the machine for 10 minutes on high pressure. Once the pressure cooking cycle has finished, depressurize completely using the quick release method.

Allow the stock to cool slightly, then strain off the liquid and set it aside for the chowder. Discard the spent vegetable matter once it's cooled enough to handle.

Makes 4 cups of stock

Recipe continues . . .

For the corn stock:

4 cups water

3 cobs corn, husks removed and discarded, kernels removed and set aside for the chowder (see photo below)

½ large red onion, quartered

1 small carrot, quartered

1 small stalk celery, quartered

1 tsp black peppercorns

1 tsp kosher salt

1 bay leaf

1 serrano pepper, whole

2–3 sprigs fresh thyme and/ or sage

Remove kernels from corn cobs and use the cobs for the stock. Save corn kernels for the chowder.

To make the chowder, set the machine to sauté and add 1 tbsp of butter and the pancetta. Sauté, stirring frequently, for 3–4 minutes or until the pancetta is lightly browned.

Add the red onion, celery root, green pepper, and salt, and stir well. Sauté for 3–4 minutes to get the juices flowing.

Stir in the white wine. Add the flour and stir well to avoid lumps. Add 1 cup of the corn stock and stir it in well.

Add the remaining corn stock and the potatoes. Stir to combine, and secure the lid.

Set the machine for 6 minutes on high pressure. Once the pressure cooking cycle has finished, depressurize completely using the quick release method.

Remove the lid and set the machine to sauté.

Add the cream, followed by the corn kernels, and allow to come nearly to a boil. Turn off the machine and stir in 2 tbsp of butter and the chopped parsley. Serve with freshly ground pepper.

Makes 8 cups

Note: You can use chicken stock, vegetable stock, or water if you don't have the gusto to make the corn stock.

For the chowder:

1 tbsp butter

4 oz pancetta, finely diced (about ½ cup)

½ large red onion, diced

1 cup diced celery root

½ medium green bell pepper, diced

1 tsp kosher salt

¼ cup white wine

2 tbsp all-purpose flour

4 cups corn stock (see Note)

2 medium red potatoes, diced

½ cup 35% cream

2 cups reserved corn kernels (about 3 cobs' worth)

2 tbsp butter

¼ cup chopped fresh parsley

freshly ground black pepper

Beef and Barley Soup

A successful beef and barley soup needs perfectly cooked barley, tender morsels of beef, and a nice rich broth to bring it all together. This recipe does all that. Comfort food at its best.

Set the machine to sauté and add the butter, onion, carrot, celery, leek, salt, and nutmeg. Season to taste with freshly ground black pepper.

Sauté for 5–6 minutes, stirring frequently, until the vegetables are soft and beginning to brown.

Add the beef and continue to cook, stirring frequently, for 2 minutes.

Add the white wine to cool down the pot, and stir in the tomato paste and thyme. Sauté for an additional 2 minutes.

Add the beef stock and barley and stir.

Secure the lid and set the machine for 20 minutes on high pressure, allowing for a 10-minute natural release before completely depressurizing the pot.

Remove the lid, stir in the parsley, and serve.

Makes 8 cups

2 tbsp butter

1 medium onion, diced

1 medium carrot, diced

1 stalk celery, diced

1 medium leek, white and light green sections only, halved lengthwise, washed well, and diced

2 tsp kosher salt

pinch nutmeg

freshly ground black pepper

1 lb stewing beef, cut into ¼-inch cubes

¼ cup white wine

1 tbsp tomato paste

2 tsp chopped fresh thyme

5 cups beef stock (page 138)

⅓ cup barley

¼ cup chopped fresh parsley

Clam Chowder

This delicious chowder is best served with a crusty sourdough or rye bread with lots of butter. It's a great start to a seafood supper and will keep you warm on a winter's eve. Baby clams are fine to use, and they're readily available, but to take this chowder to the next level, keep your eyes open for canned or frozen bar clams or surf clams.

Set the machine to sauté and add the butter, red onion, celery, leek, thyme, and salt. Season to taste with freshly ground black pepper and stir well. Sauté for 3–4 minutes to get the juices flowing.

Add the flour and stir vigorously to avoid lumps. Add 1 cup of the water and stir it in well.

Stir in the remaining 3 cups of water, then add the potatoes, the clams, and the clam juice. Stir to combine, making sure nothing sticks to the bottom of the pot, and secure the lid.

Set the machine for 15 minutes on high pressure, allowing for a 10-minute natural release before completely depressurizing the pot.

Remove the lid, stir in the cream, and serve.

Makes 12 cups

¼ cup butter

1 large red onion, diced

3 stalks celery, diced

1 leek, white and green sections only, halved lengthwise, washed well, and diced

1 tbsp chopped fresh thyme

2 tsp kosher salt

freshly ground black pepper

¼ cup all-purpose flour

4 cups water

5 medium Yukon gold potatoes, diced

one 5-oz (142 g) can baby clams, with juices

1 cup 35% cream

Cheeseburger Soup

All the usual suspects are here. Carrots, onions, and celery are the basics in many soups, but this one's special. The fresh tomato garnish and lots of grated cheese make for an ooey-gooey experience. So easy and fast, it will have you singing "Cheeseburger in Paradise."

Set the machine to sauté and allow it to preheat for 4–5 minutes.

Add the butter and allow it to melt. Add the beef, dispersing it evenly into the bottom of the pot. However tempting, don't stir it up for about 5 minutes. This will allow the beef to caramelize to a nice golden brown on one side.

After the first stir, continue to sauté for an additional 2–3 minutes, stirring frequently to break up the meat into smaller pieces.

Add the salt, tomato paste, mustard, and garlic, and stir well to combine, for about 1 minute.

Add the celery, carrot, red onion, and potatoes, and stir well to combine.

Add the beef stock, passata, bay leaf, Worcestershire sauce, and hot sauce. Stir well and secure the lid.

Set the machine for 10 minutes on high pressure. Once the pressure cooking cycle has finished, depressurize completely using the quick release method.

Remove the lid and ladle the soup into bowls. Garnish with a healthy handful of grated cheese, green onions, and chopped tomato.

Makes 7 cups

1 tbsp butter

1½ lb ground beef

1 tsp kosher salt

2 tsp tomato paste

2 tsp Dijon mustard

2 cloves garlic, minced

1 stalk celery, diced

1 medium carrot, diced

1 small red onion, diced

2 medium Yukon gold
potatoes, cut into
½-inch dice

4 cups beef stock (page 138)

1½ cups passata

1 bay leaf

2 tsp Worcestershire sauce

3 shakes hot sauce

6 oz grated Cheddar cheese

2 green onions, chopped

2 tomatoes, quartered, seeds
removed, diced

Creamy Mushroom and Barley Soup

This stick-to-the-ribs recipe is a quick winter warmer, especially when served with a hunk of crusty bread and some good-quality salted butter. There aren't many ingredients, and there's little work needed to get this soup going. When it's ready, you'll wonder how it can be so good. Spoiler alert: it's the butter and the cream.

Set the machine to sauté and allow it to preheat for about 2 minutes.

Add the butter, celery, leek, carrot, thyme, and salt, and cook, stirring frequently, for 5 minutes.

Stir in the barley, followed by the mushrooms, and continue to cook for 2 more minutes.

Add the flour and stir well.

Add 1 cup of the chicken stock and stir well to incorporate the flour. Add the remaining stock and stir.

Secure the lid and set the machine for 15 minutes on high pressure. Allow for a 10-minute natural release before completely depressurizing the pot.

Remove the lid, and set the machine to sauté. Stir in the cream and bring to a simmer, about 3 minutes.

Turn off the machine and serve.

Makes 9 cups

Note: Get everything in the pot before heading out to shovel the snow. You'll be happy you did!

2 tbsp butter

2 stalks celery, diced

1 large leek, white and light green sections only, halved lengthwise, washed well, and diced

1 medium carrot, diced

1 tbsp chopped fresh thyme

2 tsp kosher salt

1 cup pearl barley

1½ lb white button mushrooms, diced

1 tbsp all-purpose flour

2 quarts chicken stock

1 cup 35% cream

Cabbage Roll Soup

There's a fine line between lazy and genius. No matter which side you think this recipe falls on, it's delicious. Enjoy all the homey flavours without all the toothpicks.

Set the machine to sauté and allow it to preheat for about 4–5 minutes.

In a large bowl, season the ground beef with paprika, salt, and freshly ground black pepper, mixing the meat well to distribute the seasoning evenly.

Add the ghee to the pot and allow it to melt. Add the beef, dispersing it evenly into the bottom of the pot. However tempting, don't stir it up for about 5 minutes. This will allow the beef to caramelize to a nice golden brown on one side.

After the first stir, continue to sauté for an additional 5 minutes, stirring frequently to break up the meat into smaller pieces.

Once all the juices have reduced and the beef starts to sizzle again, add the celery, onions, and garlic to the pot. Sauté for 2 minutes, stirring frequently to make sure nothing sticks to the bottom.

Add the beef stock, diced tomatoes, passata, Worcestershire sauce, and bay leaf, and stir well to combine. Add the cabbage and the rice and stir again.

Secure the lid and set the machine for 15 minutes on high pressure. Once the pressure cooking cycle has finished, depressurize completely using the quick release method.

Remove the lid, stir everything well, and allow to cool for 5–10 minutes before ladling the soup into bowls.

Serve with sour cream and freshly chopped chives or green onions.

Makes 16 cups

Notes: For a rounder, richer flavour, replace half the ground beef with ground pork or ground veal.

This recipe is easily halved.

2 lb ground beef (see Note)

1 tbsp paprika

1 tbsp kosher salt

½ tbsp freshly ground black pepper

1 tbsp ghee

2 stalks celery, cut into ½-inch dice

2 medium onions, cut into ½-inch dice

2 cloves garlic, minced

3 cups beef stock (page 138)

one 28-oz (796 ml) can diced tomatoes

3 cups passata

1 tbsp Worcestershire sauce

1 bay leaf

¼ medium cabbage, roughly diced (about 3 cups)

½ cup converted rice, rinsed and drained

sour cream and chopped fresh chives or green onions, for garnishing

Lentil Soup with Bacon and Tomato Salsa

Simple soup made super easy. Now say that five times fast! This recipe works because of the bacon and tomato salsa you add at the end, providing tang and texture.

Set the machine to sauté and add the bacon and the water. Sauté for 6–8 minutes or until the bacon is evenly browned and crisp. Remove the bacon with a slotted spoon and transfer to a plate or bowl lined with a paper towel. Leave the fat in the pot.

Add the celery, onion, carrot, leek, and salt. Season to taste with freshly ground black pepper.

Sauté for 5–6 minutes, stirring frequently, until the vegetables are soft and beginning to brown.

Add the tomato paste and continue to cook, stirring frequently, for 2 more minutes.

Add the lentils, chicken stock, and bay leaf, and stir.

Secure the lid and set the machine for 15 minutes on high pressure, allowing for a 10-minute natural release before completely depressurizing the pot.

In a small bowl, mix together the bacon, green onions, tomatoes, and lime juice, and season to taste with salt and freshly ground black pepper. Reserve for garnishing.

Remove the lid and stir in the chopped fresh herbs.

Ladle soup into bowls and serve immediately, topped with bacon and tomato salsa.

Makes 10–12 cups

Note: You can use regular streaky bacon if you don't have double-smoked available.

6 slices (about 6 oz) double-smoked bacon, diced (see Note)
2 tbsp water
1 stalk celery, diced
1 large onion, diced
1 medium carrot, diced
1 leek, white and light green sections only, halved lengthwise, washed well, and diced
2 tsp kosher salt
freshly ground black pepper
2 tbsp tomato paste
1½ cups dried green or brown lentils, rinsed and drained
8 cups chicken stock
1 bay leaf
2 green onions, finely sliced
2 medium tomatoes, quartered, seeds removed, cut into ¼-inch dice
½ lime, juiced (1½ tbsp)
kosher salt
freshly ground black pepper
¼ cup chopped fresh herbs (such as chives and parsley)

Beef Pho

It's all in the broth. Traditionally, pho is one of those dishes that takes a long time to make – with the beef simmering for many hours for the right texture. This version needs only a few steps to build all the flavours. The recipe borrows from the French in more ways than one. (Or is it the other way around?) The onion brûlée (burned onion) offers a little caramel colour to the broth along with added flavour.

Set the machine to sauté and add the cardamom pods, cloves, star anise, cinnamon stick, coriander seeds, and fennel seeds. Stir frequently for 3–4 minutes to toast the spices, drawing their flavours to the forefront. Remove the spices and set aside to cool slightly before transferring them to a small spice bag (see Note).

While the pot is still hot, place the onion, cut side down, on the bottom of the pot. Sear the onion for 3–4 minutes to caramelize. Remove the onion and set aside.

While the pot is still hot, add the peanut oil and sear the oxtail for 2–3 minutes per side to get a nice brown colour on the meat.

Once the oxtail is browned, add the water, the seared onion, spice bag, ginger coins, brisket, Thai bird chili, fish sauce, and salt.

Secure the lid and set the machine for 45 minutes on high pressure, allowing for a 40-minute natural release before completely depressurizing the pot.

Remove the lid, then remove and discard the spice bag and the onion.

Recipe continues . . .

Notes: If you don't have a spice bag, a do-it-yourself tea bag (made for loose-leaf tea) works well.

There are two sides to a brisket – the point (fattier end) and the flat (leaner). This recipe uses the flat.

7 cardamom pods

4 whole cloves

2 whole star anise

1-inch piece cinnamon stick

1 tsp coriander seeds

1 tsp fennel seeds

1 large onion, peel on, halved

2 tbsp peanut oil

1 lb oxtail

10 cups water

3 ginger coins (fresh ginger, unpeeled, cut across the grain into ¼-inch rounds)

1½-lb piece beef brisket (the flat end) (see Note)

1 red Thai bird chili, whole

1 tbsp fish sauce

1 tbsp kosher salt

Continued from previous page

Transfer the brisket to a cutting board and slice thinly. Set aside.

Arrange the oxtail, brisket slices, and vermicelli into bowls. Ladle the soup into the bowls and serve with raw beef slices, Thai basil, culantro, bean sprouts, and lime wedges.

Makes 10 cups of broth (serves 6–8)

Notes: Vermicelli can be cooked ahead of time and stored in cold water until needed. You can use the pressure cooker to boil water and cook the noodles. Use any width of noodle you like.

Thinly sliced beef can be found fresh or frozen at Asian markets.

- 1 package (about 1 lb) vermicelli, cooked (see Note)
- ½ lb thinly sliced raw beef (inside round) (see Note)
- 1 bunch fresh Thai basil
- 1 bunch fresh culantro (also known as sawtooth cilantro or long cilantro – can substitute cilantro)
- 4 cups bean sprouts
- 1 lime, cut into wedges

Mulligatawny Soup

The name means "pepper-water." This recipe was borrowed from India by the British, and it's been in a constant state of change over many years. The red lentils and the basmati rice give the dish body while the hot chili keeps you coming back for more. Double up the chili pepper if you want a version that pays homage to the name.

Set the machine to sauté. Add the ghee, onion, leek, celery, apple, Thai bird chili, thyme, ginger, garam masala, turmeric, and salt, and season to taste with freshly ground black pepper.

Sauté for 3–4 minutes, stirring frequently.

Add the chicken thighs and continue to cook, stirring frequently, for 2 minutes.

Add the chicken stock, coconut cream, lime juice, lentils, and rice, and stir well. Add the lemongrass and lime leaf.

Secure the lid and set the machine for 6 minutes on high pressure.

Once the pressure cooking cycle has finished, depressurize completely using the quick release method.

Remove the lid and serve.

Makes 8 cups

Note: Coconut cream is similar to coconut milk, but it contains less water and has a denser texture. If coconut cream is not available, you can use coconut milk instead.

2 tbsp ghee

1 small onion, finely diced

1 leek, white and light green sections only, halved lengthwise, and sliced in half-rings

1 stalk celery, diced

1 McIntosh apple, peeled and diced, stem and seeds removed

1 red Thai bird chili, minced

1 tbsp chopped fresh thyme

1 tbsp chopped fresh ginger

2 tsp garam masala

1 tsp turmeric

2 tsp kosher salt

freshly ground black pepper

1 lb chicken thighs, boneless and skinless, thinly sliced

4 cups chicken stock

1 cup coconut cream (see Note)

1 lime, juiced (3 tbsp)

¼ cup split red lentils (dried), rinsed and drained

¼ cup basmati rice, rinsed and drained

one 2-inch piece lemongrass

1 lime leaf

Bahamian Souse

The locals eat this dish, pronounced "sowse," for breakfast. Enjoy a completely uncomplicated and nourishing start to your day, even if it's already noon.

Place the chicken pieces into a sealable container. Add the bay leaves, thyme sprigs, allspice, clove, serrano pepper, lime juice, salt, and rum, and season to taste with freshly ground black pepper.

Turn the chicken pieces around in the marinade until evenly coated. Refrigerate for 2–4 hours or overnight.

Place the potatoes, poblano peppers, celery, onion, and carrot into the pot.

Place the marinated chicken pieces, with marinade, into the pot and pour in the water. Give everything a good stir and add the Scotch bonnet pepper. Secure the lid.

Set the machine for 15 minutes on high pressure, allowing for a 20-minute natural release before completely depressurizing the pot.

Remove the lid and serve with lime wedges and salt (see Note).

Makes 8 cups (serves 4–6)

Note: If you like it hot, break open the Scotch bonnet after cooking, to release the heat!

one 3 ½- to 4-lb chicken, cut into 8 pieces (see photo on page 199)
2 bay leaves
10 sprigs fresh thyme
5 whole allspice, ground in a mortar and pestle
1 clove, ground in a mortar and pestle or spice grinder
1 serrano pepper, chopped
1 lime, juiced (3 tbsp)
2 tsp kosher salt
1 oz dark rum
freshly ground black pepper
4 small Yukon gold potatoes, quartered
2 medium poblano peppers, cut into 1-inch dice
2 stalks celery, cut into 1-inch pieces
1 medium onion, cut into 8 wedges
1 large carrot, cut into ½-inch rounds
6 cups water
1 Scotch bonnet pepper, whole
1 lime, cut into wedges
kosher salt

Tortilla Soup

Let's taco 'bout this legendary Mexican soup. Mildly spicy from the poblano and jalapeño peppers, it is cooled down with fresh avocado and queso fresco garnishes.

Place the dried black beans into a container large enough to hold double the volume. Cover with 2 cups of water and refrigerate for a minimum of 12 hours, although 24 hours is ideal.

Set the machine to sauté and add the ghee, garlic, onion, poblano pepper, jalapeño pepper, celery, red pepper, and salt, and sauté for 5–6 minutes, stirring frequently, until the vegetables are soft and beginning to brown.

Drain and rinse the black beans and add them to the pot and stir.

Add the cornmeal, diced tomatoes, and chicken stock, and stir.

Secure the lid and set the machine for 15 minutes on high pressure.

Once the pressure cooking cycle has finished, depressurize completely using the quick release method.

Remove the lid and serve with avocado, lime wedges, tortilla chips, queso fresco, and fresh cilantro as garnish.

Makes 8 cups

1 cup dried black beans

2 tbsp ghee

3 cloves garlic, minced

1 medium onion, diced

1 poblano pepper, diced

1 jalapeño pepper, finely diced

1 large stalk celery, diced

½ red bell pepper, diced

2 tsp kosher salt

¼ cup cornmeal

one 28-oz (796 ml) can diced tomatoes

3 cups chicken stock

Suggested garnishes:

1 avocado, diced

1 lime, cut into wedges

2 cups tortilla chips

1 cup queso fresco, crumbled

½ bunch fresh cilantro sprigs

Tuscan Bean Soup

White beans – whether navy beans, cannellini, or great northern beans – have been a part of Tuscan cooking forever. In the early days, white beans were funnelled into an empty Chianti bottle that had the basket portion removed. Filled with water and olive oil, the bottle was placed next to the fading fire overnight. In the morning, the beans were cooked and ready to use in the dishes being prepared for the day. A romantic tale, but let's use the electric pressure cooker to cook the beans to perfection and get this meal on the table.

Place the dried white beans into a container large enough to hold double the volume. Cover with 2 cups of water and refrigerate for a minimum of 12 hours, although 24 hours is ideal.

Set the machine to sauté and add the olive oil, garlic, carrots, celery, onion, and salt, and sauté for 5–6 minutes, stirring frequently, until the vegetables are soft and beginning to brown.

Drain and rinse the white beans and add them to the pot and stir.

Add the white wine, diced tomatoes, and chopped kale, and stir.

Add the chicken stock and herbs, and stir.

Secure the lid and set the machine for 20 minutes on high pressure.

Once the pressure cooking cycle has finished, depressurize completely using the quick release method.

Remove the lid, stir in the Parmesan cheese, and serve.

Makes 8 cups

1 cup dried white beans

2 tbsp olive oil

4 cloves garlic, minced

2 medium carrots, thinly sliced into quarter-rounds

2 stalks celery, diced

1 large onion, diced

2 tsp kosher salt

½ cup white wine

one 28-oz (796 ml) can diced tomatoes

3–4 cups chopped kale (ribs removed)

3 cups chicken stock

½ cup chopped fresh herbs (such as basil and oregano)

½ cup grated Parmesan cheese

Fancy Cauliflower Soup

A distinguished version of plain, old-fashioned cauliflower soup, this one requires an extra step at the beginning to make the garnish. But those looks of amazement you get from family and guests will make it worth the effort. Basmati rice is used to thicken the soup and gives it its velvety texture. From the cruciferous family of vegetables, cauliflower is high in Vitamin C and antioxidant rich.

To make the garnish, take a quarter of the cauliflower and cut it into bite-sized or smaller pieces. Roughly chop the rest and set aside for the soup.

Set the machine to sauté and allow it to preheat for 4–5 minutes.

Add 2 tbsp of butter to the pot, followed by the smaller portion of cauliflower, half the diced jalapeño pepper, the red onion, and ½ tsp of salt. Sauté for 3–4 minutes to get some colour and to soften the cauliflower.

Add the coriander seeds, turmeric, and garam masala, and quickly stir to combine. Add the water and the lemon juice to cool down the pot. Cook for 1 minute and turn off the machine. Stir in the green onions and the parsley, and transfer the contents of the pot to a bowl for garnishing later.

To make the soup, return the pot to the machine. Add 2 tbsp of butter, the sweet onion, celery, remaining cauliflower, remaining jalapeño pepper, and 1 tsp of salt.

Stir in the white wine, rice, and stock, and secure the lid.

Set the machine for 8 minutes on high pressure. Once the pressure cooking cycle has finished, depressurize completely using the quick release method.

Remove the lid, add the cream, and purée the soup with a hand blender until smooth.

Ladle the soup into bowls and garnish with the cauliflower goodness you made at the beginning.

Makes 8 cups

1 medium cauliflower, core removed
2 tbsp butter
1 jalapeño pepper, halved, seeds removed, diced
1 small red onion, thinly sliced
½ tsp kosher salt
1 tsp coriander seeds, freshly ground
¾ tsp turmeric
½ tsp garam masala
¼ cup water
½ lemon, juiced (2 tbsp)
2 green onions, thinly sliced
2 tbsp fresh parsley, chopped
2 tbsp butter
1 medium sweet onion, diced
1 large stalk celery, diced
1 tsp kosher salt
¼ cup white wine
⅓ cup basmati rice, rinsed and drained
4 cups chicken or vegetable stock
½ cup 35% cream

Chicken Noodle Soup

Say goodbye to canned soup. This wholesome, nourishing dish is just what the doctor ordered. Your electric pressure cooker makes it a snap to prepare.

Set the machine to sauté and add the celery, carrots, onion, leek, butter, salt, and nutmeg. Season to taste with freshly ground black pepper.

Sauté for 5–6 minutes, stirring frequently, until the vegetables are soft and beginning to brown.

Add the water, chicken thighs, tomato, and bay leaf, and stir.

Secure the lid and set the machine for 10 minutes on high pressure, allowing for a 5-minute natural release before completely depressurizing the pot.

Remove the lid and set the machine to sauté. Once the soup begins to simmer, add the noodles and simmer for 3–5 minutes (according to package instructions).

Once the noodles are cooked, turn off the machine and stir in the chopped fresh herbs.

Makes 10 cups

Note: Double up on flavour by using chicken stock in place of the water.

2 stalks celery, thinly sliced across the grain

2 small carrots, sliced into ¼-inch-thick rounds

1 medium onion, diced

1 leek, white and light green sections only, halved lengthwise, washed well, and cut against the grain into ½-inch-thick slices

2 tbsp butter

2 tsp kosher salt

pinch nutmeg

freshly ground black pepper

6 cups water (see Note)

6 chicken thighs, boneless and skinless, cut into ½-inch slices

1 large tomato, diced

1 bay leaf

1½ cups soup noodles (thin, quick-cooking egg noodles)

¼ cup chopped fresh herbs (such as chives and parsley)

Beef Stock

Beef Stock

Beef stock was invented in the interest of extracting every last bit of flavour out of expensive proteins. Making beef stock out of bones and scraps is a wonderful way to add a layer of flavour to soups, stews, and saucy beef dishes. Typically a beef stock would simmer on the stove for 8 hours or so, but your electric pressure cooker does the job fast and efficiently. If you use a lot of beef stock, try making a remouillage (second stock) – a stock made from bones that have already been used to make stock. It's much weaker than the original but can be used to make your next beef stock – a richer alternative to starting with water. You can make a remouillage by simply refilling the pot with water and running a 10-minute pressure cycle.

Set the machine to sauté and allow it to preheat for 4–5 minutes.

Place the onion, cut side down, on the bottom of the pot, along with the garlic. Sear for 3–4 minutes to blacken.

Place the rest of the ingredients into the pot, stir, and secure the lid.

Set the machine for 1 hour on high pressure, allowing for a full natural release. This step could take 30–60 minutes, depending on the pot and where it is positioned.

Remove the lid and allow to cool 5–10 minutes before straining. Discard the spent bone and vegetable matter and keep the glorious broth, refrigerated, for 2 weeks, or freeze for up to 3 months.

Makes 12 cups

Note: As an option, once the stock is strained, reduce the volume of liquid by boiling to a concentrate – about 25% of the original volume (for example, 4 cups boiled down to 1 cup) – then freeze in small quantities. It's like having frozen bouillon cubes.

1 large onion, only the outer layer of peel removed, halved

3 cloves garlic, peel on

2–2½ lb beef bones and scraps, cut small enough to fit in the pot

2 plum tomatoes, halved

1 large carrot, skin on, cut into chunks

1 stalk celery, cut into chunks

10 sprigs fresh parsley

3 quarts cold water

2 bay leaves

2 tsp kosher salt

1 tsp black peppercorns

Bone Marrow Herb Butter

Making bone marrow herb butter may take some planning, but it's that little extra time that leads to something extraordinary. Intended for garnishing the meat lover's chili (page 141), this fortified butter can also be used to top your grilled meats for a restaurant-style experience at home.

Season the bones to taste with salt and freshly ground black pepper.

Cut six 12- by 12-inch pieces of aluminum foil. Place two pieces of foil, one on top of the other, on a flat surface.

Place one bone onto the centre of the foil sheets. Bring each of the edges up to the top of the bone, where you can then pinch all the sides together to form a tightly sealed pouch. Repeat with remaining foil squares and bones.

Pour the water into the pot and insert the trivet. Place the bones, standing up, on the trivet.

Secure the lid and set the machine for 45 minutes on high pressure. Once the pressure cooking cycle has finished, depressurize completely using the quick release method.

Carefully remove the bones from the pot and unwrap the foil. Use caution because there will be hot fat inside, which you want to keep for the chili.

Remove the marrow from the centre of each bone, using a small spoon. Transfer to a bowl and smash all the marrow with a fork.

Add the butter, ½ tsp of salt, herbs, and lemon zest to the marrow, and mix well.

Refrigerate until needed, up to 2 weeks, or freeze for up to 3 months.

Makes about 1 cup

3 large beef marrow bones
   (about 2–2½ lb total)
kosher salt
freshly ground black pepper
1½ cups water
⅔ cup butter, softened
½ tsp kosher salt
½ cup chopped fresh herbs
   (such as parsley, oregano,
   and sage)
1 tsp lemon zest

Meat Lover's Chili

You can't please everyone all the time, but you sure can please the dedicated carnivores in your life with this meaty concoction. The different meats create the layers of flavour essential to a good chili con carne. The bone marrow herb butter garnish sets this recipe apart from the crowd.

Place the dried kidney beans into a container large enough to hold double the volume. Cover with 2 cups of water and refrigerate for a minimum of 12 hours, although 24 hours is ideal.

Set the machine to sauté and allow it to preheat for about 4–5 minutes. Add the beef fat or butter and allow it to heat up for 30 seconds. Add the stewing beef, dispersing it evenly into the bottom of the pot. However tempting, don't stir it up for about 5 minutes. This will allow the beef to caramelize to a nice golden brown on one side.

After the first stir, sauté for an additional 2–3 minutes, stirring frequently. Then remove the seared stewing beef from the pot and add the ground beef and chorizo. Treat these meats the same way, allowing them to caramelize for about 5 minutes before stirring. After stirring the first time, stir frequently for 2–3 minutes to break up the meat into smaller pieces. It's OK to have a few chunky bits.

Add the red onion, red pepper, green pepper, celery root, garlic, tomato paste, thyme, chili powder, and salt to the pot. Season to taste with freshly ground black pepper. Sauté for 4–5 minutes, stirring frequently.

Add the diced tomatoes, beef stock, soy sauce, Worcestershire sauce, and soaked, drained, and rinsed kidney beans. Stir well to combine.

Return the stewing beef to the pot. Secure the lid and set the machine for 20 minutes on high pressure, allowing for a 10-minute natural release before completely depressurizing the pot.

Remove the lid, and set the machine to sauté. Whisk in the roux ½ tbsp at a time, until you reach the desired consistency. Turn off the machine after 2 minutes.

Serve with a dollop of bone marrow herb butter.

1 cup dried kidney beans

2 tbsp beef fat (left from cooking the marrow bones, page 139) or butter

1 lb stewing beef, cut into ½-inch cubes

1½ lb ground beef

½ lb chorizo sausage, casings removed

1 large red onion, diced

1 red bell pepper, diced

½ green bell pepper, diced

¾ cup diced celery root

3 cloves garlic, minced

2 tbsp tomato paste

1 tbsp chopped fresh thyme

2 tbsp chili powder

2 tsp kosher salt

freshly ground black pepper

one 28-oz (796 ml) can diced tomatoes

3 cups beef stock (page 138)

1 tbsp soy sauce

1 tbsp Worcestershire sauce

1–2 tbsp roux (page 19)

bone marrow herb butter (page 139) for garnishing

Makes 4 quarts

Meatball Sandwich

Tender meatballs in an uncomplicated tomato sauce, presto – a fast and easy way to feed the whole family. You can make the meatballs a day ahead for extra ease at mealtime. The food processor yields fine enough pieces of celery, garlic, and onions and will save you time chopping.

Place the ground beef into a large bowl and add the celery, garlic, onion, egg, bread crumbs, oregano, salt, and paprika. Season to taste with freshly ground black pepper. Mix well (hands are best) until uniform in consistency.

Form the mixture into tightly packed balls, about 2 oz each, for about 20 in total.

Set the machine to sauté.

Add the beef stock and the crushed tomatoes and bring to a simmer, stirring frequently to make sure nothing sticks to the bottom of the pot.

Add the meatballs to the sauce, gently stirring them in to coat completely.

Secure the lid and set the machine for 15 minutes on high pressure, allowing for a 10-minute natural release.

Remove the lid and serve the meatballs on buns, with the grated mozzarella and garnished with parsley.

Serves 6–8

2 lb ground beef

2 stalks celery, minced in a food processor on pulse

2 cloves garlic, minced in a food processor on pulse

1 medium onion, minced in a food processor on pulse

1 large egg

½ cup dry bread crumbs

1 tbsp chopped fresh oregano

2 tsp kosher salt

1 tsp paprika

freshly ground black pepper

1 cup beef stock (page 138)

one 28-oz (796 ml) can crushed tomatoes

6-8 submarine or hoagie buns (each 6-8 inches long)

1 cup grated mozzarella cheese

fresh parsley for garnishing

Meat Sauce

An essential recipe for everyone's repertoire. Great for making lasagna or served simply with noodles. Tomatoes react very well when pressure cooked, turning a few ingredients into a rich and delicious sauce ready in a fraction of the time you'd expect for flavours this big.

Set the machine to sauté and allow to it preheat for 4–5 minutes.

Add the olive oil and allow it to heat up for 30 seconds. Add the beef, dispersing it evenly into the bottom of the pot. However tempting, don't stir it up for about 5 minutes. This will allow the beef to caramelize to a nice golden brown on one side.

After the first stir, continue to sauté for an additional 5 minutes, stirring frequently to break up the meat into smaller pieces.

Add the garlic, serrano pepper, and salt, and sauté for 30 seconds. Add the red wine to cool down the pot, followed by the celery, onion, and carrot. Stir frequently for 2–3 minutes to get the cooking started.

Add the passata and bring to a simmer, stirring frequently to make sure nothing sticks to the bottom of the pot.

Stir in the herbs, season to taste with freshly ground pepper, and secure the lid.

Set the machine for 15 minutes on high pressure, allowing for a 10-minute natural release before completely depressurizing the pot.

Remove the lid and allow to cool uncovered so the excess moisture will evaporate.

Refrigerate for up to 7 days.

Makes 6 cups

2 tbsp olive oil

1½ lb ground beef

4 cloves garlic, finely chopped

1 serrano pepper, seeds and stem removed, finely chopped

2 tsp kosher salt

¼ cup red wine

2 stalks celery, finely chopped

1 large onion, finely chopped

1 medium carrot, finely chopped

3 cups passata

½ cup chopped fresh herbs (such as parsley, oregano, and basil)

freshly ground black pepper

Classic German-Style Beef Rouladen

This is the classic version, but you can also fill the roll with other ingredients: herbs, portobello mushrooms, ham, sausage meat, green beans, peppers, sun-dried tomatoes, olives . . . and on and on. Try this version first. After that, the sky's the limit.

Place the thin beef slices on a flat surface (each piece will be a rough rectangular shape). Sort the slices so the narrow sides are facing toward you.

Smear 1 tsp of the mustard evenly over each piece of beef. Place a strip of bacon on an angle across the meat, with one end starting at the close left side of the meat across to the back right of the rectangle. This way, there will be bacon in every bite.

Place the pickles and carrot sticks together, parallel to the short side of the rectangle closest to you. Start rolling by folding the close edge over the carrots and pickles, and roll tightly until you reach the far edge. Secure with a tooth-pick. Repeat with the remaining beef slices.

Recipe continues . . .

6 pieces (about 4 oz each) thinly sliced beef rump or round

2 tbsp Dijon mustard

6 thin slices double-smoked bacon

1 large or 2 small kosher pickles, cut into spears

1 large carrot, cut into 4-inch sticks (just like the pickles)

kosher salt

freshly ground black pepper

pinch paprika

1 tbsp all-purpose flour

2 tbsp canola oil

1 medium onion, diced

½ cup diced celery root

1 medium carrot, diced

1 tbsp tomato paste

½ cup red wine

2 cups beef stock (page 138)

1 bay leaf

2 tbsp roux (page 19)

1 tbsp chopped fresh chives (optional)

Set the machine to sauté and allow it to preheat for 4–5 minutes.

Season the rolls with salt, freshly ground black pepper, and paprika to taste. Coat rolls in flour, gently shaking off the excess.

Add the canola oil to the pot and allow it to heat up for a minute before adding the rolls. Work in 2 or 3 batches so you don't overcrowd the searing surface. Sear on all sides and remove from the pot. Repeat with remaining rolls.

Once the rolls are seared and removed, add the onion, celery root, and diced carrot to the pot, stirring frequently for 3–4 minutes.

Stir in the tomato paste and brown a little, continuing to stir, for 1 minute.

Add the red wine and reduce while using a wooden spoon to release the caramelized juices from the bottom of the pot.

Add the beef stock and bay leaf, stir well, and bring to a simmer.

Add all the rolls back to the pot and secure the lid.

Set the machine for 20 minutes on high pressure. Allow for a 10-minute natural release before completely depressurizing the pot.

Remove the rouladen from the pot and cover loosely with foil.

Set the machine to sauté and bring the sauce to a simmer. Add the roux, ½ tbsp at a time, and whisk into the sauce. Simmer for about 30 seconds and turn off the machine. Season with salt and freshly ground black pepper to taste.

Return the rouladen to the pot and roll them around in the sauce before serving. Garnish with chives, if desired.

Serves 6

Beef Pot Roast Stroganoff

The term *stroganoff* refers to a Russian beef dish finished with sour cream. Many variations have morphed over the years to include mushrooms and onions and such, as in this version. The bottom blade roast, cut from the shoulder, is perfect for pot roast. Even better, this cut is perfect for the electric pressure cooker, as it is typically cooked slow and low to break down the different muscles that come together.

Set the machine to sauté and allow it to preheat for 4–5 minutes.

Season the beef with salt and pepper to taste on all sides, pressing the seasonings into the meat so they adhere.

Add the canola oil to the pot and then add the beef. Sear for 3–5 minutes on each side (2 sides). Remove the beef and set aside.

Add the onion, carrot, celery, herbs, and chili flakes, and stir well to release any bits stuck to the bottom of the pot. Sauté for 4–5 minutes, until the ingredients are glossy and starting to brown.

Stir in the mustard and the tomato paste, then sauté for 1 minute before adding the white wine, beef stock, and mushrooms. Stir well, making sure nothing sticks to the bottom of the pot.

Return the seared beef to the pot and secure the lid.

Set the machine for 60 minutes on high pressure. Allow for a 20-minute natural release before completely depressurizing the pot.

Recipe continues . . .

- 2 lb beef bottom blade roast
- 2 tsp kosher salt
- freshly ground black pepper
- 2 tbsp canola oil
- 1 large onion, diced
- 1 large carrot, diced
- 1 large stalk celery, diced
- 2 tbsp chopped fresh herbs (such as rosemary, thyme, and sage)
- ½ tsp chili flakes
- ¼ cup Dijon mustard
- 2 tbsp tomato paste
- ½ cup white wine
- ½ cup beef stock (page 138)
- 1 lb button mushrooms, sliced
- 2 tbsp roux (page 19)
- 2 green onions, chopped
- ½ cup sour cream

Continued from previous page

Remove the lid and carefully remove the roast from the pot. Transfer to a cutting board for carving.

Set the machine to sauté and bring the sauce to a boil. Turn off the machine.

Immediately whisk in the roux, half a tablespoon at a time, until the desired consistency is reached. The sauce will continue to thicken as it cools. Stir in the green onions and you're done.

Slice the roast against the grain as best as possible. (The grain will change directions as you go because of the different muscles that make up the roast.)

Serve with the sauce, and sour cream on the side.

Serves 6–8

Les Short Ribs

The name "short rib" comes, unsurprisingly, from the size of the bone, which is much shorter than a whole beef rib. It's cut from the brisket or chuck section of the cow, closer to the front leg than the spine. The bones are wider than the ones attached to a rib-eye steak. The cut requires a long, slow cooking process to break down the membranes and connective tissues. Or at least it used to.

Set the machine to sauté and allow it to preheat for 4–5 minutes.

Season the short ribs on all sides with salt. Season to taste with freshly ground black pepper.

Add the ghee to the pot, allowing it to heat up, about 30 seconds. Sear the short ribs on at least two sides, two or three chunks at a time. Overcrowding will cool the pot below searing temperature, so take your time.

Once the short ribs have all been seared, remove them from the pot. Add the carrot, onions, celery root, and garlic cloves. Sauté, stirring frequently, for 6–8 minutes or until the vegetables have browned a little.

Add the chopped fresh herbs, tomato paste, and mustard, and stir for another minute. Add the red wine and continue to cook for 2–3 minutes to let the wine reduce by at least half, while stirring to make sure nothing sticks to the bottom of the pot.

Stir in the beef stock, add the bay leaf, and return the seared short ribs to the pot, nestling them into the sauce.

Secure the lid and set the machine for 40 minutes on high pressure, allowing for a 10-minute natural release before completely depressurizing the pot.

Remove the lid and remove the short ribs. Use one of the fat-skimming techniques described on pages 22–23.

Use a hand blender to purée right in the pot. All the cooked vegetables and juices become the sauce.

Serves 4–5

4 lb (4–5 pieces) beef short ribs, about 4-inch bone
2 tsp kosher salt
freshly ground black pepper
3 tbsp ghee
1 large carrot, cut into 1-inch pieces
2 medium onions, roughly diced
1 cup diced celery root
4 cloves garlic (whole), peeled
2 tbsp chopped fresh herbs (such as parsley, rosemary, and thyme)
2 tbsp tomato paste
1 tbsp Dijon mustard
1 cup red wine
1 cup beef stock (page 138)
1 bay leaf

Korean-Inspired Short Ribs

The short ribs you normally find in a Korean barbecue restaurant have been cut into thin strips across the bone, resembling what you may know as button ribs or Miami ribs. This recipe uses a traditional short rib cut because the EPC is so fast at turning this cut into soft and delectable pieces of beef. The resulting sweet and salty sauce is umami-packed and sticky – very similar to Korean kalbi sauce.

Set the machine to sauté, and allow it to preheat for 4–5 minutes.

Season the short ribs on all sides with freshly ground black pepper, to taste.

Add the peanut oil to the pot, allowing it to heat up, about 30 seconds.

Sear the short ribs on at least two sides, two or three at a time. Overcrowding will cool the pot below searing temperature, so take your time.

Once the short ribs have all been seared and removed from the pot, add the onion, garlic, ginger, and red pepper powder. Sauté, stirring frequently, for 2–3 minutes, to soften the onion.

Add the lime juice, soy sauce, and rice vinegar, and stir for another minute to make sure nothing sticks to the bottom of the pot.

Return the seared short ribs to the pot.

Secure the lid and set the machine for 40 minutes on high pressure, allowing for a 10-minute natural release before completely depressurizing the pot.

Recipe continues . . .

4 lb (4–5 pieces) beef short ribs, about 4-inch bone
freshly ground black pepper
3 tbsp peanut oil
1 medium onion, thinly sliced
6 cloves garlic, minced
3 tbsp chopped fresh ginger
1 tbsp Korean red pepper powder
½ lime, juiced (1½ tbsp)
½ cup soy sauce
½ cup unseasoned rice vinegar
⅓ cup light brown sugar
2 tbsp cornstarch
2 tbsp water
4 green onions, chopped
1 tbsp sesame seeds
1 tbsp sesame oil

Continued from previous page

Remove the lid and remove the short ribs.

Use one of the fat-skimming techniques described on pages 22–23.

Once the fat is removed, bring the sauce to a simmer using the sauté function.

Whisk in the brown sugar and cook for 1 minute.

In a small bowl, mix the cornstarch with the water. Whisk into the simmering sauce and turn off the machine.

Add the green onions, sesame seeds, and sesame oil. The sauce is ready to pour onto the short ribs, or add the short ribs back to the pot to keep warm.

Serves 4–5

Beef Carnitas

If it's Taco Tuesday, great! If it's not, make it anyway. Guajillo peppers, which are on the lower end of the heat scale, add a sweet and smoky flavour to many Mexican dishes.

Season the beef with the cumin seeds, salt, and ground chili, and freshly ground pepper to taste, rubbing the mixture into the meat so it adheres.

Set the machine to sauté and allow it to preheat for 4–5 minutes.

Add the ghee to the pot, then add the pieces of beef. Sear for 4–5 minutes on each side (2 sides). Remove the beef and set aside.

Add the garlic, green onions, onion, poblano pepper, and sliced almonds, and stir well. Sauté for 4–5 minutes, stirring frequently.

Add the tequila and continue to stir to release any bits stuck to the bottom of the pot.

Add the passata and beef stock and bring to a simmer, stirring frequently to make sure nothing sticks to the bottom of the pot. Return the seared beef to the pot and secure the lid.

Recipe continues . . .

2-lb beef bottom blade roast, cut in half
2 tbsp cumin seeds
2 tsp kosher salt
2 dried guajillo chilies, ground in a spice grinder
freshly ground black pepper
2 tbsp ghee
4 cloves garlic, minced
4 green onions, chopped
1 small onion, diced
1 poblano pepper, diced
2 tbsp sliced almonds
1 oz tequila
1 cup passata
1 cup beef stock (page 138)
2 tbsp roux (page 19)
½ cup chopped fresh cilantro

Continued from previous page

Set the machine for 60 minutes on high pressure, allowing for a 10-minute natural release before completely depressurizing the pot.

Remove the lid and carefully remove the beef from the pot. Transfer to a bowl for shredding. Shred the beef using a pair of forks, 2 pairs of tongs, or any other way you choose.

Set the machine to sauté and bring the sauce to a boil. Immediately whisk in the roux, half a tablespoon at a time, until the desired consistency is reached. Turn off the machine. Remember that the sauce will continue to thicken as it cools. Stir in the fresh cilantro just before serving.

If serving with tacos, mix about half the sauce into the shredded beef, leaving the rest for dipping. Place the beef in soft corn or flour tortillas and top with all the taco garnishes you've ever dreamed of.

If serving with rice, add all of the sauce to the meat.

Serves 8

Hungarian Beef Goulash

Goulash is all about the onions. This is a rare recipe in this book where you need to run two pressure cooking cycles. The onions in goulash traditionally need to be cooked for a long time, breaking down and providing the rich colour needed for the sauce. The machine cuts down the cooking time while still reaching the proper doneness of the onions. Salt potatoes are the traditional accompaniment (see pages 88–89).

Set the machine to sauté and add the butter, onions, and salt. Sauté, stirring frequently, for 4–5 minutes to get the onions to release enough water for a successful pressure cook.

Secure the lid and set the machine for 5 minutes on high pressure. Once the pressure cooking cycle has finished, depressurize completely using the quick release method.

Remove the lid and set the machine to sauté.

Sauté the onions for 25–30 minutes. Stir frequently while the water evaporates, and very frequently once the onions start to caramelize. You want a dark brown colour; the onions will barely resemble onions when they're done (see photo below).

Add the paprika, marjoram, caraway seeds, garlic, lemon zest, tomato paste, and red wine vinegar. Stir well to combine.

Stir in the beef stock and the beef and bring to a simmer before securing the lid.

Set the machine for 30 minutes on high pressure, allowing for a 15-minute natural release before completely depressurizing the pot.

Remove the lid and serve with salt potatoes.

Serves 4–8

¼ cup butter
2 lb onions, sliced
   (about 8 medium)
2 tsp kosher salt
3 tbsp paprika
1 tbsp dried marjoram
1 tsp caraway seeds, ground in
   a mortar and pestle or spice
   grinder
3 cloves garlic, minced
zest of 1 lemon (about 2 tsp)
2 tbsp tomato paste
2 tbsp red wine vinegar
2 cups beef stock (page 138)
2 lb stewing beef, cut into
   1-inch cubes

Caramelized onions

Veal Osso Buco

Italian for "bone with a hole," osso buco was conceived to make the most of the underused lower section of the leg or shin. Traditionally served with risotto Milanese, this recipe will also go well with salt potatoes (page 89) or roasted garlic mashed potatoes (page 83). Don't forget to get a small spoon and scoop out the marrow from the hole in the bone.

Set the machine to sauté and allow it to preheat for 4–5 minutes.

Season the veal on all sides with salt and freshly ground black pepper to taste.

Add the olive oil to the pot, allowing it to heat up, about 30 seconds. Sear the veal on both sides, one or two at a time. Overcrowding will cool the pot below searing temperature, so take your time. Remove the veal from the pot and set aside.

Add the onion, carrot, celery root, fresh herbs, and garlic. Sauté, stirring frequently, for 3–4 minutes.

Stir in the tomatoes, the white wine, and the bay leaf. Bring to a simmer, about 1–2 minutes, stirring to make sure nothing sticks to the bottom of the pot.

Return the seared veal shanks to the pot, nestling them into the sauce. It may be a tight fit.

Secure the lid and set the machine for 30 minutes on high pressure, allowing for a 10-minute natural release before completely depressurizing the pot.

Remove the lid and carefully remove the veal shanks.

Set the machine to sauté and bring the juices to a simmer. Whisk in the roux, half a tablespoon at a time, until the desired consistency is reached, remembering that the sauce will thicken as it cools. Turn off the machine.

Return the shanks to the sauce and garnish with fresh parsley. The osso buco is ready to serve.

Serves 4–6

four 12–14-oz veal shank
   cross-sections
   (1½–2 inches thick)
2 tsp kosher salt
freshly ground black pepper
2 tbsp olive oil
1 large onion, diced
1 large carrot, diced
1½ cups diced celery root
2 tbsp chopped fresh herbs
   (such as thyme and sage)
2 cloves garlic, minced
4 cups cherry or grape
   tomatoes, halved
½ cup white wine
1 bay leaf
1–2 tbsp roux (page 19)
2 tbsp chopped fresh parsley

Mole Braised Pork

Pork Pozole

Pozole refers to a Mexican-style hominy stew with countless variations. Back in the day, dried hominy kernels were slowly simmered over a fire, but the EPC now makes short work of the job.

Place the dried hominy corn into a container large enough to hold double the volume. Cover with 2 cups of water and refrigerate for a minimum of 12 hours, although 24 hours is ideal. Drain and rinse before using.

Grind together the cumin and coriander seeds and the peppercorns using a mortar and pestle or spice grinder.

Place the pork in a large bowl and season with the ground spices and salt. Mix well to evenly coat the pork.

Set the machine to sauté and allow it to preheat for 4–5 minutes. Add the ghee and allow it to melt, which will happen pretty quickly. Add the seasoned pork, dispersing it evenly into the bottom of the pot. However tempting, don't stir up the meat for about 5 minutes. This will allow the pork to caramelize to a nice golden brown on one side.

After the first stir, add the onion, celery, poblano peppers, jalapeño pepper, garlic, ginger, and oregano. Continue to sauté for 4–5 minutes, stirring frequently.

Add the stock, tomatillos, and hominy corn, and stir well.

Secure the lid and set the machine for 18 minutes on high pressure. Allow for a 5-minute natural release before completely depressurizing the pot.

Remove the lid, give the pozole one final stir, and serve with cilantro leaves, avocado, sour cream, radish slices, and jalapeño slices.

Makes about 10 cups

Note: Canned tomatillos can be substituted. Drain and hand crush before using.

1 cup dried white hominy corn

1 tsp cumin seeds

1 tsp coriander seeds

½ tsp black peppercorns

1½- to 1¾-lb pork shoulder, boneless, cut into 1-inch cubes

2 tsp kosher salt

2 tbsp ghee

1 large sweet onion, diced

2 stalks celery, diced

2 poblano peppers, diced

1 jalapeño pepper, finely diced

4 cloves garlic, minced

2 tbsp chopped fresh ginger

2 tbsp chopped fresh oregano

3 cups chicken stock or water

4 tomatillos, outer husks removed, washed, and diced (see Note)

Suggested garnishes:

fresh cilantro leaves

diced avocado

sour cream

radish slices

jalapeño pepper slices

Pork and Beans 2.0

This is a pork and beans recipe that truly puts the pork first. The fall-off-the-bone, juicy baby back ribs and white beans in a rich BBQ-style sauce will make everyone smile. Serve with buttered toast.

Place the white beans into a container large enough to hold double the volume. Cover with 3 cups of water and refrigerate for a minimum of 12 hours, although 24 hours is ideal. Drain and rinse before using.

In a small bowl, mix together the paprika, chili powder, cumin, coriander, and 1 tsp of salt. Rub this spice mix over the rib pieces, using your hands to press the spices evenly onto the meat (see photo on next page). Set aside. You can do this step up to 24 hours before you're ready to start cooking.

In a small bowl or measuring cup, mix together the beer, brown sugar, Worcestershire sauce, tomato paste, molasses, and mustard. Set aside.

Set the machine to sauté and add the bacon and the 1 tbsp of water. Sauté, stirring for 3–4 minutes, to allow the bacon fat to render out before adding the onion, red pepper, garlic, thyme, 1 tsp of salt, and freshly ground black pepper to taste.

Sauté, stirring frequently, for 8–10 minutes, lightly browning the onion and pepper. Add the soaked, drained, and rinsed beans and the beer mixture and bring to a simmer, stirring frequently.

Recipe continues . . .

Notes: White beans are on the smaller side and can be called navy beans or great northern beans.

If you're a beer lover, experiment with different beers such as porter or maple-flavoured varieties. If not, you can use water or chicken stock in place of the beer.

1½ cups dried white beans (see Note)
1 tbsp paprika
½ tbsp chili powder
1 tsp ground cumin
1 tsp ground coriander
1 tsp kosher salt
1 rack (2½–3 lb) pork baby back ribs, membrane removed (see photo on page 166), cut in single bones (about 12 bones)
1 cup dark beer (see Note)
2 tbsp brown sugar
2 tbsp Worcestershire sauce
2 tbsp tomato paste
1 tbsp fancy molasses
1 tbsp Dijon mustard
6 slices bacon, diced
1 tbsp water
1 medium onion, diced
1 medium red bell pepper, diced
3 cloves garlic, minced
1 tbsp chopped fresh thyme
1 tsp kosher salt
freshly ground black pepper

Continued from previous page

Place the ribs evenly over the top of the beans, but don't stir them in.

Secure the lid and set the machine for 20 minutes on high pressure. Allow for a 10-minute natural release before completely depressurizing the pot.

Remove the lid and remove the ribs to serving plates. Stir up the beans and serve alongside the ribs. Voilà!

Serves 4–6

Peel back and remove the membrane before seasoning.

Mole Braised Pork

This is a basic mole sauce recipe for pork intended for your next taco, burrito, or rice bowl. The tamarind provides tang, and the unrefined cane sugar, known as panela, gives an earthy sweetness.

In a spice grinder, grind together the chili, cumin seeds, and coriander seeds. Add the ground cinnamon and set the spice mix aside.

Set the machine to sauté and allow it to preheat for 4–5 minutes.

Place the pork pieces in a large bowl and season with salt and freshly ground black pepper to taste.

Add the peanut oil to the pot, allowing it to heat up, about 30 seconds. Sear the pork pieces on at least two sides, two or three at a time. Overcrowding will cool the pot below searing temperature, so take your time.

Once the pork has all been seared and removed from the pot, add the garlic, onion, diced polano pepper, raisins, tamarind paste, chocolate, thyme, and the spice mix. Sauté, stirring frequently, for 3–4 minutes.

Stir in the tomatoes and the chicken stock, making sure nothing is stuck to the bottom of the pot.

Return the seared pork pieces to the pot, nestling them into the sauce.

Secure the lid and set the machine for 15 minutes on high pressure, allowing for a 5-minute natural release before completely depressurizing the pot.

Remove the lid. Mix up the pork and the sauce to encourage the meat to break apart.

Stir in the grated panela and chopped cilantro and serve.

Serves 6–8

1 dried guajillo chili

1 tsp cumin seeds

1 tsp coriander seeds

pinch ground cinnamon

1½–2 lb pork shoulder, cut into ¼-lb chunks

2 tsp kosher salt

freshly ground black pepper

2 tbsp peanut oil

4 cloves garlic, chopped

1 medium onion, diced

1 poblano pepper, diced

¼ cup raisins

2 tbsp tamarind paste

½ oz unsweetened dark chocolate, chopped

2 tbsp chopped fresh thyme

2 medium tomatoes, chopped

½ cup chicken stock

1 tbsp grated panela

¼–½ cup chopped fresh cilantro

Honey Mustard Pork Rib Tartine with Fennel Slaw

The electric pressure cooker is so good at fall-off-the-bone ribs that this recipe is a no-brainer. A tartine is the original French version of the open-faced sandwich. A step outside the normal barbecue flavours, this honey mustard version, accompanied by the punchy flavours of fennel and fresh tarragon, will be an instant favourite at your house.

In a small bowl, mix together the Dijon mustard, whole-grain mustard, honey, and apple cider, and pour over the rib sections, making sure to coat all sides. Refrigerate until you're ready to cook, for at least 1 hour and up to 24 hours.

Set the machine to sauté and add the butter, sweet onions, garlic, and salt, and season to taste with freshly ground black pepper. Sauté for 4–5 minutes, stirring frequently to soften the onions and garlic.

Add the ribs, layered as evenly as possible, and all the marinade. Secure the lid.

Set the machine for 30 minutes on high pressure. Once the pressure cooking cycle has finished, depressurize completely using the quick release method.

While the ribs are in the pot, make the slaw.

Recipe continues . . .

For the ribs:

2 tbsp Dijon mustard

2 tbsp whole-grain mustard

2 tbsp honey

⅓ cup apple cider

1 rack (2½–3 lb) pork baby back ribs, about 12 bones, membrane removed (see photo, page 166), cut into 3-bone sections

2 tbsp butter

2 large sweet onions, roughly diced

6 cloves garlic

2 tsp kosher salt

freshly ground black pepper

Continued from previous page

To make the slaw, place the shaved fennel, apple, and red onion into a bowl and toss with the olive oil, apple cider vinegar, tarragon, and salt. Season to taste with freshly ground black pepper. Set aside.

Remove the lid and transfer the ribs to a plate. Carefully remove the bones, using a pair of tongs and a fork. The bones should wiggle free without clinging too much to the meat (see Note).

Use a hand blender to purée the sauce right in the pot.

Serve the ribs on a slice of bread and a handful of arugula. Finish with slaw on top and a side of sauce.

Serves 4

Notes: A mandoline is the best tool for making the slaw. It's great for thinly shaving many types of fruits and vegetables. It's also very dangerous, so pay close attention if using this tool.

Once the bones are removed, you can return the rib meat to the pot and keep it warm in the sauce until the crew is ready to eat.

For the slaw (see Note):

1 small head fennel, fronds trimmed off, quartered, cored, and shaved

1 Granny Smith apple, quartered, cored, and shaved

1 small red onion, thinly shaved, soaked in ice water for 5 minutes, drained

2 tbsp olive oil

2 tbsp apple cider vinegar

2 tbsp chopped fresh tarragon

1 tsp kosher salt

freshly ground black pepper

To finish:

4 slices of good bread, such as sourdough, Calabrese, or Italian loaf

fresh arugula for garnishing

Kakuni Braised Pork Belly Bahn Mi

Kakuni is a Japanese braised pork dish sometimes served with rice or in soup. Here it's turned into a Vietnamese-style sandwich with fresh vegetables and a sweet, spicy sauce. This recipe may sound exotic, but it's surprisingly easy to put together, and everyone can build their own sandwich.

In a small bowl, mix together the garlic, mirin, soy sauce, peppercorns, star anise, ginger, red pepper powder, and ground cinnamon.

Place the pork into a sealable container and pour in the marinade, making sure the pork is evenly coated on all sides (see Note). Refrigerate for 12–24 hours.

Place the pork belly and the marinade into the pot and add the water. Secure the lid and set the machine for 40 minutes on high pressure.

Once the pressure cooking cycle has finished, depressurize completely using the quick release method.

Remove the lid and carefully remove the pork. There will be a fair amount of fat floating on the sauce once it settles. Use one of the fat-skimming techniques described on pages 22–23.

Allow to cool 10 minutes or more before slicing. (See photo on page 173.)

Set the machine to sauté and whisk in the brown sugar. Simmer for 3–4 minutes and turn off the machine.

Recipe continues . . .

Note: Resealable bags are great for marinating. If you squeeze the air out, the meat will be fully submerged in the marinade, which will enhance the effect and shorten marinating times.

2 cloves garlic, minced

2 tbsp mirin (sweet rice wine)

2 tbsp soy sauce

1 tbsp Szechuan or black peppercorns, coarsely ground in a mortar and pestle or spice grinder

1 whole star anise, coarsely ground in a mortar and pestle or spice grinder

1 tbsp chopped fresh ginger

1 tbsp Korean red pepper powder

¼ tsp ground cinnamon

One 1-lb piece pork belly, skinless, cut in half if you need it to fit in the pot better

1 cup water

2 tsp dark brown sugar

Continued from page 171

For the slaw, place the salad greens, carrot, radish, cucumber, rice wine vinegar, salt to taste, fish sauce, and cilantro into a bowl. Toss well right before you make the sandwich for maximum freshness and crunch.

Open the buns and put in the pork belly slices and drizzle with the sauce. Serve the remaining sauce on the side.

Divide the fresh vegetable slaw evenly into the buns on top of the pork.

Pass out the sandwiches and get eating!

Serves 4–8

For the slaw:

2 cups thinly sliced salad greens (romaine, iceberg, or napa cabbage)

1 medium carrot, cut into matchsticks

½ small daikon radish, cut into matchsticks

½ cucumber, cut into matchsticks

2 tbsp seasoned rice wine vinegar

kosher salt to taste

1 tsp fish sauce

½ cup roughly chopped fresh cilantro

To finish:

1 baguette, cut to make 4–8 sandwich buns

Peameal Bacon Roast

This unique brining process is fabled to have started in Toronto's St. Lawrence Market over a century ago, when wet-brined pork loins were rolled in crushed yellow peas to lengthen the shelf life. Today we make the meal from corn because of its popularity and price. This recipe has few ingredients and is simple to make; however, the prep involves math, and you'll need an accurate kitchen scale.

Weigh your pork loin in grams. Let's refer to this as the pork weight (PW). The cure ingredients are calculated as follows:
Kosher salt is 2% of the PW, or PW x 0.02
Curing salt is 1% of the PW, or PW x 0.01
Brown sugar is 0.5% of the PW, or PW x 0.005

The perfect size loin for the pot is about 1200 grams. In this case, PW = 1200 g. Therefore, PW x 0.02 = 24 g (kosher salt); PW x 0.01 = 12 g (curing salt); and PW x 0.005 = 6 g (brown sugar).

Place the pork on a flat surface and pierce repeatedly with a fork on all sides, about 20 times.

In a bowl, mix together the weighed salt, curing salt, and brown sugar and rub the mixture evenly over the whole surface of the pork. Place the pork into a resealable bag and add the ½ cup of water (or beer, if using). Remove as much air from the bag as you can. Gently massage the meat through the bag for a minute to combine all the ingredients. Refrigerate for 48–72 hours, agitating at least once a day.

Remove the pork from the brine, rinse well under cold running water, and pat dry. Coat the cured pork evenly on all sides with the cornmeal.

Place the 1 cup of water in the pot and then put in the trivet. Place the peameal bacon on the trivet and secure the lid.

Set the machine for 25 minutes on high pressure. Once the pressure cooking cycle has finished, depressurize completely using the quick release method. Do not remove the lid. Allow to rest for 10 minutes (machine off) with the lid on.

Remove the lid and carefully remove the bacon from the pot. Transfer to a cutting board for carving. Cut into thin slices and serve as the centrepiece of your brunch – or get out the lettuce, tomato, and mayo for a great sandwich.

one 1.2-kg (1200 grams) piece
   centre-cut pork loin
2% by weight kosher
   salt = 24 grams
1% by weight curing
   salt = 12 grams (see Note)
0.5% by weight light brown
   sugar = 6 grams
½ cup water or beer
½ cup cornmeal
1 cup water for steaming

Note: Get curing salt (a.k.a. pink salt) from your butcher. This salt gives the peameal its signature colour. (Do not confuse with Himalayan pink salt, which is a fancy rock salt.)

Serves 8

Creamy Potatoes and Peameal Bacon

A belly-warmer side dish for dinner or beside your eggs for breakfast or brunch. The vinegar plays a vital role in this dish. Give it a taste before and after adding it to see why. No need to be fussy with the potatoes – a lazy peel is fine, leaving a little skin on there for flavour.

Set the machine to sauté and allow it to preheat for 2 minutes.

Add the butter and let it melt. Then add the onion, thyme, and salt, and stir. Season to taste with freshly ground black pepper and nutmeg. Sauté, stirring frequently, for 6–7 minutes or until the onion is softened and lightly browned.

Add the water and stir, scraping to release any brown bits stuck to the bottom of the pot.

Add the diced potatoes and bacon, and stir.

Secure the lid and set on high pressure for 3 minutes. Once the pressure cooking cycle has finished, depressurize completely using the quick release method.

Remove the lid, immediately turn on the sauté function, and stir in the cream. Turn the machine off once the liquid comes to a boil (about 2 minutes).

Wait another 3–4 minutes for the liquid to stop boiling, making sure to stir gently from time to time to prevent scorching.

Stir in the white vinegar and serve.

Serves 4–6

Note: The "Canadian bacon" you find in grocery stores in the United States is not peameal bacon. It's also not a Canadian invention, despite the name. Don't give up if you can't find it. You can make your own using the brining recipe for peameal bacon (page 175).

2 tbsp butter

1 medium onion, cut into ½-inch dice

1 tbsp chopped fresh thyme

2 tsp kosher salt

freshly ground black pepper

freshly grated nutmeg

1¼ cups water

6 medium potatoes, cut into ½-inch dice

1 lb raw peameal bacon, homemade (page 175) or store-bought, cut into ½-inch dice

½ cup 35% cream

1 tbsp white vinegar

Saucy Pulled Pork on a Bun

It's Wednesday and you just got home from work, but that doesn't mean you can't have homemade pulled pork for dinner. Yes, this dish is traditionally smoked for hours and hours to break down the fats and connective tissues in the pork shoulder, but today the electric pressure cooker will have it ready for you in a little over an hour. While slow-and-low smoked pork shoulders may reign supreme in the Carolinas, don't let anyone tell you this isn't a tasty sandwich.

Place the pork into a large bowl and season with the paprika, salt, cumin seeds, and freshly ground black pepper to taste. Rub the seasonings into the meat to give it an even coat. You can do this up to a day in advance.

Set the machine to sauté and allow it to preheat for 4–5 minutes.

Add the ghee to the pot and allow it to melt and coat the bottom.

Sear the pork on all sides and remove from the pot. If the machine isn't big enough, work in batches so you don't over-crowd the searing surface.

Once the pork is seared and removed, add the onion, garlic, and the water to the pot. Use a flat-bottomed wooden spoon to scrape off the crispy pork bits stuck to the bottom of the pot. Continue to sauté for 3–4 minutes to get the juices flowing.

Add the passata, apple cider vinegar, and Worcestershire sauce, and stir well to combine.

Place the pork pieces in the sauce and secure the lid. Set the machine for 70 minutes on high pressure.

Sometime near the end of the cooking process, prepare the slaw.

Recipe continues . . .

4-lb boneless pork shoulder, cut into four 1-lb chunks, skin on or off

1 tbsp paprika

2 tsp kosher salt

1 tsp cumin seeds

freshly ground black pepper

2 tbsp ghee

1 medium onion, diced

3 cloves garlic, roughly chopped

2 tbsp water

1 cup passata

¼ cup apple cider vinegar

3 tbsp Worcestershire sauce

¼ cup packed dark brown sugar

Continued from page 177

Place the shredded cabbage, grated carrot, and green onions into a big bowl.

Pour in the apple cider vinegar and canola oil, and season with sugar, salt, and freshly ground black pepper to taste. Mix together and set aside.

Once the pressure cooking cycle has finished, allow for a 10-minute natural release before completely depressurizing the pot. Remove the lid.

Carefully transfer the pork pieces to a bowl and skim the fat off the top of the sauce. (See fat separation techniques on pages 22–23.)

Set the machine to sauté and bring the sauce to a boil. Whisk in the brown sugar, allowing it to completely dissolve, and turn off the machine.

Remove any skin and unwanted fat from the pork and discard them. Use a pair of forks to help break apart the remaining pork.

Transfer the pork back into the sauce and stir to make sure the sauce coats all the meat.

Serve on fresh buns with slaw.

Serves 8

For the slaw:

¼ **cabbage, shredded (about 4 cups)**

1 **medium carrot, grated**

2 **green onions, finely sliced**

3 **tbsp apple cider vinegar**

2 **tbsp canola oil**

½ **tsp sugar**

½ **tsp kosher salt**

freshly ground black pepper

To finish:

8 **fresh big buns**

Pork Belly Kimchi Stew

Also known as kimchi jjigae, this stew can be made with a variety of proteins, but pork and tofu together is the most popular combination. Kimchi, a spiced and fermented cabbage, is a staple in Korean cuisine, either as an ingredient or a garnish, served alongside a variety of other popular garnishes called pan chan. You'll find it at Korean and other Asian markets. A quick-to-put-together marinade on the pork belly overnight takes this recipe to the next level.

In a small bowl, mix together the soy sauce, mirin, red pepper powder, fish sauce, sesame oil, and 5 sprigs chopped cilantro. Add the pork belly slices and gently mix to coat all the pieces of pork. Cover and refrigerate for 12–24 hours. (See marinating note, page 171.)

Set the machine to sauté and allow it to preheat for 4–5 minutes. Add the peanut oil and the mushrooms. Sauté for 8–10 minutes, stirring occasionally. Over-stirring will prevent caramelization, so don't overdo it.

Stir in the onion, garlic, and ginger, and continue to sauté for 1–2 minutes. Add the kimchi and the pork belly, including all the marinade, and stir well. Stir in the stock and secure the lid.

Set the machine for 10 minutes on high pressure. Once the pressure cooking cycle has finished, depressurize completely using the quick release method.

Remove the lid and stir in the tofu, ¼ cup of cilantro, and green onion. Place the lid back on and wait 2–3 minutes for the tofu to warm through before serving.

Serves 4–6

Notes: You could try making your own kimchi, although the smell of slowly fermenting cabbage isn't for the faint of heart.

Tofu comes in all sorts of textures, from extra soft to super firm. The higher the water content, the softer the tofu, and the more likely that it will break apart during cooking. Firmer styles of tofu have higher amounts of protein and fat because a greater amount of water has been removed.

¼ cup soy sauce

3 tbsp mirin (sweet rice wine)

1 tbsp Korean red pepper powder

2 tsp fish sauce

1 tsp sesame oil

5 sprigs fresh cilantro, coarsely chopped, stems and all

12 oz pork belly, skinless, cut into ½- x ½- x 2-inch slices

2 tbsp peanut oil

4 large king oyster mushrooms, bottoms trimmed, cut in half lengthwise, and thinly sliced

1 large sweet onion, thinly sliced

3 large cloves garlic, minced

2 tbsp chopped fresh ginger

2 cups prepared kimchi (see Note)

3 cups chicken or vegetable stock

½ lb firm tofu, cut into ½-inch dice (see Note)

¼ cup chopped fresh cilantro

1 green onion, chopped

Ancho Chicken Carnitas

POULTRY

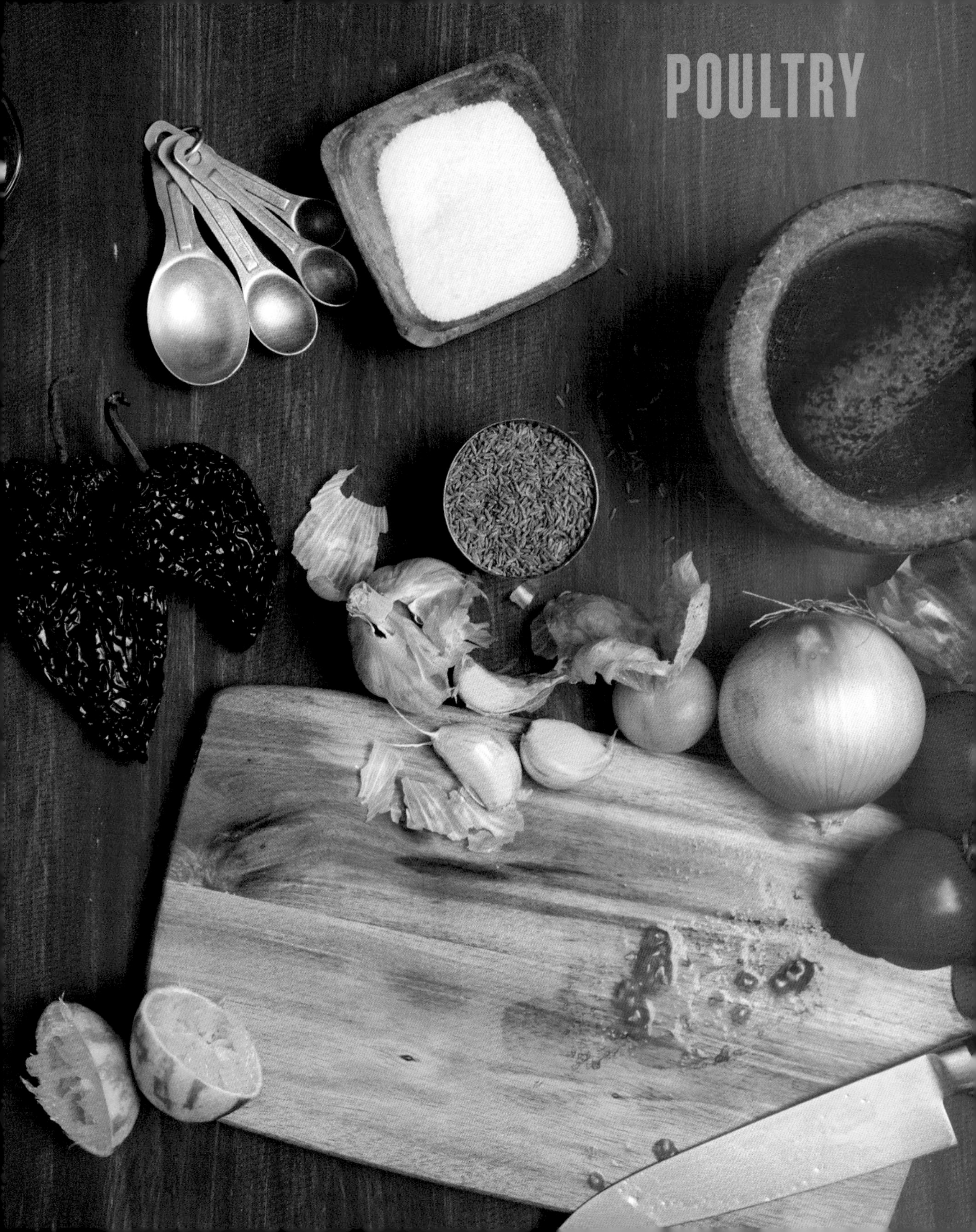

Chicken Stock

If you ever need to convince friends to get an electric pressure cooker, make them this rich chicken stock bursting with flavour. If you want more richness, add a few chicken feet (available at some Asian markets) to the mix. They're loaded with natural gelatin, which leaves a lip-smacking stickiness.

Place all the ingredients into the pot. Secure the lid.

Set the machine for 1 hour on high pressure, allowing for a full natural release. This could take 30–60 minutes, depending on the pot and where it is positioned.

Remove the lid and allow to cool 5–10 minutes before straining. Discard the spent bone and vegetable matter and keep the glorious broth, refrigerated, for 2 weeks, or freeze for up to 3 months.

Makes 12 cups

Notes: This stock freezes well, packed in small portions for easy access.

Save raw chicken and random vegetable scraps, freeze them, and make this stock when you've accumulated a sufficient amount.

- 2–2½ lb chicken bones and/or parts, cut small enough to fit in the pot
- 1 large carrot, skin on, cut into chunks
- 1 large onion, only the outer layer of peel removed, quartered
- 1 stalk celery, cut into chunks
- 1 leek, halved lengthwise, washed well, and cut into 2- or 3-inch pieces
- 10 sprigs fresh parsley
- 3 quarts water
- 1 tsp black peppercorns
- 2 bay leaves
- 2 tsp kosher salt

Chicken Cacciatore

Many original versions of cacciatore were made with rabbit and wild mushrooms from the forest. This rustic version goes nicely with potatoes, noodles, or rice.

Season the chicken with salt and freshly ground black pepper.

Set the machine to sauté and allow it to preheat for 4–5 minutes.

Add the olive oil to the pot and allow it to heat up for a minute. Sear the chicken on both sides, about 3–4 minutes per side, and remove from the pot. You may want to do this in 2 batches so you don't overcrowd the searing surface, allowing the pot to return to full heat before starting the second batch.

Once the thighs are seared and removed from the pot, add the thyme, rosemary, chili flakes, celery, carrot, onion, and all the mushrooms. Stir frequently for 3–4 minutes.

Stir in the red wine and return the seared chicken to the pot, using a wooden spoon to coax some of the meat under the sauce.

Secure the lid and set the machine for 15 minutes on high pressure. Once the pressure cooking cycle has finished, depressurize completely using the quick release method. Do not remove the lid.

Allow to rest for 5 minutes (machine off) with the lid on.

Remove the lid and serve.

Serves 4

Notes: If there is too much fat for your liking, use one of the fat-skimming techniques described on pages 22–23.

This recipe will work with rabbit legs, if you're into that sort of thing.

- 4 (about 4 oz each) chicken thighs, bone in, skin on
- 1 tbsp kosher salt
- 1 tsp freshly ground black pepper
- 2 tbsp olive oil
- 1 tbsp chopped fresh thyme
- ½ tbsp chopped fresh rosemary
- ½ tsp chili flakes
- 1 large stalk celery, roughly diced
- 1 medium carrot, roughly diced
- 1 medium onion, roughly diced
- 2 medium portobello mushrooms, stems removed, each cut into 8–12 wedges
- 5–6 (about 2 oz total) shiitake mushrooms, stems removed, halved
- 1–3 pieces dried porcini mushrooms, coarsely chopped (about 1 tbsp)
- ½ cup red wine

Chicken and Dumplings

The origins of this North American favourite can be traced to French Canadians during the Great Depression, when necessity dictated what was served for dinner. Today's chicken and dumplings have more to them. Vegetables and flavours round it out, making it an everyday comfort food, sure to be an instant favourite.

For the dumplings, in a large bowl, mix together the semolina, flour, chives, milk, melted butter, cheese, baking powder, and salt, and season to taste with freshly ground black pepper. Set aside.

For the stew, set the machine to sauté and add the butter, onion, celery, carrot, and salt. Sauté, stirring frequently, for 3–4 minutes, until soft but not browning.

Add the flour, stirring well to avoid lumps. Add the white wine, and stir well to let out the flour. Add the chicken stock and cream and stir.

Add the diced chicken thighs and bay leaf, and stir well to incorporate. Season to taste with freshly ground black pepper.

Scoop the dumpling batter into golf ball–sized balls (use an ice cream scoop). Place the balls evenly on top of the stew, but don't stir them in. It is important to work quickly to finish this step.

Secure the lid and set the machine for 5 minutes on high pressure, allowing for a 15-minute natural release before completely depressurizing the pot.

Remove the lid and serve garnished with chives.

Serves 4–6

For the dumplings:

½ cup semolina

½ cup all-purpose flour

¼ cup chopped fresh chives

½ cup 2% milk

⅓ cup butter, melted

2 oz grated Cheddar cheese (½ cup)

1 tsp baking powder

1 tsp kosher salt

freshly ground black pepper

For the stew:

2 tbsp butter

1 medium onion, diced

2 stalks celery, diced

1 medium carrot, diced

2 tsp kosher salt

2 tbsp all-purpose flour

½ cup white wine

1½ cups chicken stock

1 cup 35% cream

1 lb skinless, boneless chicken thighs, cut into 1-inch dice

1 bay leaf

freshly ground black pepper

2 tbsp chopped fresh chives

Chicken Saltimbocca with Potatoes

This recipe has been adapted from the classic Italian veal dish. It gets all its flavour from the prosciutto, the capers, and the sage and is perfect with a nice salad and a patio.

Place the prosciutto on a flat surface. Arrange so the short ends of each piece face toward you.

Place a sage leaf onto each prosciutto slice, followed by a chicken thigh, with the side where the skin had been facing down. Sprinkle the chopped sage over the top of the chicken, and season to taste with salt and freshly ground black pepper.

Start rolling at the close edge, rolling tightly until you reach the far edge. Secure with a toothpick. Nice rolls!

Set the machine to sauté and allow it to preheat for 4–5 minutes.

Add the olive oil to the pot and allow it to heat up for 1 minute. Place 3 of the rolls into the pot and sear on each side for 2–3 minutes, or until the prosciutto is a nice golden brown. Remove the rolls from the pot. Repeat with the remaining rolls, allowing the pot to preheat for about 1 minute before adding the next round.

Once the rolls are seared and removed, add the butter, shallots, and capers, and sauté, stirring frequently, for 2 minutes.

Add the flour and stir vigorously to incorporate. Add half the white wine and stir well to let out the flour.

Stir in the rest of the wine, followed by the chicken stock. Add the potatoes and give them a little stir into the sauce. Place the prosciutto-wrapped chicken on top and secure the lid.

Set the machine for 8 minutes on high pressure. Once the pressure cooking cycle has finished, depressurize completely using the quick release method. Do not remove the lid.

Allow to rest for 5 minutes (machine off) with the lid on. Remove the lid and serve.

Serves 4–6

6 slices prosciutto

6 large sage leaves

6 (about 3 oz each) chicken thighs, boneless and skinless

2 tbsp chopped fresh sage

kosher salt

freshly ground black pepper

6 or more toothpicks

2 tbsp olive oil

1 tbsp butter

3 large shallots, thinly sliced in rings

1 tbsp capers

½ tbsp all-purpose flour

¾ cup white wine

¾ cup chicken stock

1 lb mini potatoes, skin on, halved

Puttanesca Chicken Thighs

Feel free to look up the origins of *puttanesca*. This is a family cookbook, so we won't discuss it here. Let's just say this dish has an alluring and pungent aroma, the kind that keeps you coming back for more. Traditionally served with spaghetti.

Season the chicken with salt and freshly ground black pepper to taste.

Set the machine to sauté and allow it to preheat for 4–5 minutes.

Add the olive oil to the pot and allow it to heat up for a minute. Sear the chicken on the skin side only (about 3 minutes) and remove from the pot. Do this in 2 batches so you don't overcrowd the searing surface, allowing the pot to return to full heat before starting the second batch.

Once the thighs are seared and removed from the pot, add the garlic, onion, serrano pepper, and thyme to the pot, stirring frequently for 3–4 minutes.

Stir in the tomato paste and mustard, and stir well for 1 minute, scraping any bits off the bottom of the pot.

Add the diced tomatoes, black olives, capers, and anchovies, and stir well.

Place the seared chicken into the pot, using a wooden spoon to coax some of the meat under the sauce.

Secure the lid and set the machine for 15 minutes on high pressure. Once the pressure cooking cycle has finished, depressurize completely using the quick release method. Do not remove the lid.

Allow to rest for 5 minutes (machine off) with the lid on. Remove the lid and serve, garnished with basil.

Serves 4–6

6 (about 3–4 oz each) chicken thighs, boneless, skin on
1 tsp kosher salt
freshly ground black pepper
2 tbsp olive oil
5 cloves garlic, thinly sliced
1 small onion, sliced into half-rounds
1 serrano pepper, thinly sliced in rings
1 tbsp chopped fresh thyme
1 tbsp tomato paste
1 tbsp Dijon mustard
14 oz (398 ml) canned diced tomatoes
½ cup pitted black olives, roughly chopped
1 tbsp capers, roughly chopped
4 anchovy filets, chopped
¼ cup chopped fresh basil

Butter Chicken

A mainstream Indian classic, best served with steamed rice or naan bread, and fresh cilantro. Marinating the chicken allows the flavours to develop and permeate the meat, and the yogurt's lactic acid adds a little tenderness. Allow for the full 24 hours of marinating if you have the time.

Mix together the garlic, Thai bird chili, yogurt, lemon juice, ginger, garam masala, turmeric, and cumin. In a large bowl or sealable bag, pour the mixture over the chicken thighs and turn to coat evenly. Marinate, refrigerated, for 12–24 hours.

Set the machine to sauté and add the ghee, onion, and salt, and sauté for 6–8 minutes, stirring frequently, until the onion is fully cooked and a rich golden brown.

Add the chicken and all its marinade, followed by the passata and the cream.

Stir well, making sure nothing sticks to the bottom of the pot.

Secure the lid and set the machine for 15 minutes on high pressure, allowing for a 5-minute natural release before completely depressurizing the pot.

Remove the lid and serve with fresh cilantro.

Serves 4–6

Note: Basmati rice (page 98) would be the perfect side dish.

2 cloves garlic, minced

1 red Thai bird chili, stem and seeds removed, chopped

½ cup plain full-fat yogurt

½ lemon, juiced (2 tbsp)

1 tbsp chopped fresh ginger

2 tsp garam masala (homemade, page 219; or use store-bought)

1 tsp turmeric

1 tsp cumin seeds, ground in a mortar and pestle or spice grinder

8 (about 3 oz each) chicken thighs, boneless and skinless, quartered

2 tbsp ghee

1 medium onion, finely diced

2 tsp kosher salt

1 cup passata

1 cup 35% cream

fresh cilantro

Ancho Chicken Carnitas

A whole chicken torn to shreds in a rich, earthy ancho pepper sauce will have them coming back for more. Better stock up on tortillas. Ancho peppers are dried poblanos, and they're fairly mild in heat.

Place the chicken onto a plate or other flat surface.

Mix together half the ancho chili powder (reserving the rest for later) and all the garlic, 2 tbsp of olive oil, salt, ground cumin, lime zest, and lime juice. Rub the mix evenly over the chicken. You're fine to proceed with the recipe at this point or you can refrigerate the marinated bird for up to 24 hours.

Set the machine to sauté and add 2 tbsp of olive oil and the onions, along with the remaining ancho chili powder. Sauté, stirring frequently, for 4–5 minutes, to get a little colour.

Add the tomatillos, tomato, and chicken stock. Stir well.

Place the trivet in the pot and place the chicken on top. Add any marinade to the pot that may have dripped off the chicken. Secure the lid.

Set the machine for 30 minutes on high pressure, allowing for a 10-minute natural release before completely depressurizing the pot.

Remove the lid and transfer the chicken to a cutting board or large bowl, leaving the juices in the pot.

Set the machine to sauté and simmer the sauce for about 8–10 minutes, letting the liquid reduce and thicken up a bit. Meanwhile, shred the chicken (see photos on page 196).

Recipe continues . . .

one 3½- to 4-lb whole chicken
2 tbsp ancho chili powder,
    (about 3 whole dried chilies,
    stems removed, ground in a
    spice grinder)
3 cloves garlic, minced
2 tbsp olive oil
1 tbsp kosher salt
1 tsp cumin seeds, ground in a
    mortar and pestle or spice
    grinder
zest and juice (3 tbsp) of 1 lime
2 tbsp olive oil
2 medium onions, thinly sliced
3 medium tomatillos, husks
    removed, washed, and diced
1 large tomato, diced
½ cup chicken stock

Continued from previous page

Use a pair of forks or a pair of tongs and a fork to get the meat off the bones. Chop up as much of the skin as you like and add it to the shredded meat.

Turn off the machine when the sauce reaches the desired consistency. Fold in the shredded chicken or spoon the desired amount of sauce overtop.

Gather your favourite people and add your favourite taco accompaniments. Dinner is ready.

Serves 4–6

Note: There's more to life than tortillas. Try this dish with rice or fresh coleslaw.

Chicken Korma

This rendition of korma has Indian and Thai influences that produce a full-flavoured, rich, and creamy dish. Best served with basmati rice and a cold Pilsner. Using chicken thighs guarantees a moist and juicy result.

Grind together the corriander, cumin, and cardamom seeds using a mortar and pestle or a spice grinder.

In a small bowl, mix together the ground spices with the turmeric and cinnamon. Rub the mixture over the chicken thighs to coat evenly. The thighs are now ready to go, though they can marinate for up to a day.

Set the machine to sauté and add the ghee, garlic, ginger, onion, Thai bird chili, sliced almonds, and salt, and sauté for 5–6 minutes, stirring frequently, until the ingredients are soft and beginning to brown.

Add the chicken thighs and stir well to incorporate.

Add the chicken stock, lemongrass, lime leaf, and coconut milk. Stir well, making sure nothing sticks to the bottom of the pot.

Secure the lid and set the machine for 8 minutes on high pressure, allowing for a 5-minute natural release before completely depressurizing the pot.

Remove the lid and serve with sprigs of fresh cilantro.

Serves 4–6

1 tbsp coriander seeds

2 tsp cumin seeds

¼ tsp cardamom seeds

1 tbsp turmeric

¼ tsp ground cinnamon

6 chicken thighs
   (about 3 oz each),
   boneless and skinless,
   halved lengthwise

2 tbsp ghee

5 cloves garlic, minced

2 tbsp minced fresh ginger

1 medium onion, finely diced

1 red Thai bird chili, stem
   removed, chopped

½ cup sliced almonds

2 tsp kosher salt

¾ cup chicken stock

one 2-inch piece lemongrass

1 lime leaf

1 cup coconut milk

12 sprigs fresh cilantro

Jerk Chicken

Jamaica is well-known for its jerk chicken, and this recipe delivers the island's famous flavours to your kitchen table. Using the whole chicken with the bones makes the dish more authentic.

Place the green onions, garlic, Scotch bonnet pepper, lime juice, onion, ginger, thyme, soy sauce, rum, molasses, salt, and allspice in a food processor and pulse until there are no big chunks left. (But you don't want a smooth paste.)

Place the chicken pieces in a bowl or use a resealable bag and pour the jerk marinade over it, making sure the marinade coats all the chicken. Cover or seal and refrigerate for 24–48 hours.

Transfer the chicken to the pot, marinade included. Arrange in a single layer as best you can. Secure the lid.

Set the machine for 15 minutes on high pressure, allowing for a 5-minute natural release before depressurizing the pot completely.

Remove the lid and remove the chicken. Set the machine to sauté and bring the sauce to a boil.

In a small bowl, whisk together the cornstarch and the water, then whisk it into the jerk sauce. Turn off the machine. Serve with rice and peas (page 101), just like in the photo.

Serves 4–6

Notes: Green Scotch bonnets are less spicy than the red ones and have a lot of nice warm flavour. Don't be fooled, though. They're still fiery!

In place of the cornstarch and water, you can use 1–2 tbsp roux (page 19).

6 green onions, chopped

5 cloves garlic

1 Scotch bonnet pepper, halved, seeds removed (see Note)

1 lime, juiced (3 tbsp)

½ sweet onion, roughly diced

1-inch piece fresh ginger, peeled and sliced into ¼-inch coins

2 tbsp chopped fresh thyme

1 tbsp soy sauce

1 oz dark rum

1 tbsp fancy molasses

1 tsp kosher salt

1 tsp allspice, freshly ground

One 3½- to 4-lb chicken, cut into 8 pieces (see photo below)

1 tbsp cornstarch (see Note)

1 tbsp water

Stuffed Turkey Dinner

If you find yourself in a smaller crowd this Thanksgiving, here's the recipe for you. No need to run the oven for hours. Just take out the electric pressure cooker and start cooking. Serve alongside red wine and apple–braised red cabbage (page 59) or creamy brussels sprouts with pancetta (page 73).

Set the machine to sauté and add the butter, onion, celery, sage, and garlic. Sauté for 4–5 minutes to soften. Stir in 1 cup of chicken stock and turn off the machine. Remove half the cooked vegetable and broth mixture and place in a large bowl for the stuffing. Reserve the rest for the gravy.

To make the stuffing, add the bread, egg, and nutmeg to the bowl with the vegetable and broth mixture. Mix thoroughly.

Cut six 18-inch pieces of butcher's twine. Place two pieces of butcher's twine parallel to each other on a flat surface, a few inches apart. Place the third piece of twine across the centre of the other two pieces. (See photo below.) Reserve the remaining pieces of twine.

Season the turkey with salt and freshly ground black pepper to taste. Place one turkey thigh, skin side down, centred on top of the twine. Pack half of the stuffing into a rough patty, about the same size as the thigh, and place it on top of the turkey. Bring the ends of the twine to the top and tightly tie each string to itself so everything is held together. Use scissors to cut off any extra twine. Repeat for the second thigh. (You may have some stuffing left over.)

Recipe continues . . .

1 tbsp butter

1 medium onion, finely diced

1 stalk celery, finely diced

¼ cup chopped fresh sage

2 cloves garlic, minced

1 cup chicken stock

1½ cups (lightly packed) torn-up light sourdough bread

1 large egg

pinch nutmeg

two 1-lb turkey thighs, boneless

2 tsp kosher salt

freshly ground black pepper

¼ cup chicken stock

1–2 tbsp roux (page 19)

¼ cup chopped fresh parsley

Add the ¼ cup of chicken stock to the pot and stir in any stuffing you may have left over.

Place the trivet in the pot and put the stuffed turkey bundles on top.

Secure the lid and set the machine for 30 minutes on high pressure, allowing for a 5-minute natural release before completely depressurizing the pot.

Remove the lid and transfer the turkey roasts to a cutting board for carving. No worries if some of the stuffing fell out during the cook – it will help thicken the gravy, like an old English bread sauce.

Set the machine to sauté and bring the sauce to a simmer. Whisk in the roux, half a tablespoon at a time, until the desired consistency is reached. Remember that sauce will continue to thicken as it cools.

Turn off the machine and stir in the fresh parsley, and you're almost ready to serve. Just remove the butcher's twine and slice each roast in half, to create 4 portions. Serve with gravy from the pot.

Serves 4

Turkey Breast Fricassee

Famously described as "halfway between a sauté and a stew," turkey fricassee is just that. A quick sauté of the vegetables builds flavours and eliminates liquid. The electric pressure cooker – with some help from the vermouth – does the stewing.

Set the machine to sauté and add the butter, mushrooms, onion, zucchini, thyme, salt, and freshly ground black pepper to taste. Sauté for 5–6 minutes to get the vegetables to soften – and perhaps brown just a little.

Add the turkey and stir in the vermouth.

Secure the lid and set the machine for 5 minutes on high pressure. Once the pressure cooking cycle has finished, depressurize completely using the quick release method.

Remove the lid, set the machine to sauté, and stir in the peas and the cream.

Mix together the cornstarch and the water, stir into the simmering fricassee, and turn off the machine.

Serve with noodles or rice.

Serves 4

2 tbsp butter

4 oz button mushrooms, sliced

1 small onion, thinly sliced

1 small zucchini, sliced into
    ½-inch half-rounds

1 tbsp chopped fresh thyme

1 tsp kosher salt

freshly ground black pepper

1 lb turkey breast, cut against
    the grain into ½-inch slices

2 oz dry vermouth

½ cup peas (freshly shucked
    or frozen)

¼ cup 35% cream

1 tbsp cornstarch

1 tbsp water

Turkey Chili

A lighter, lower-fat chili when compared to the meat lover's version (page 141), this recipe also packs a lot of flavour. A good variety of vegetables goes into the dish, and the red lentils provide the right texture. A crowd pleaser extraordinaire.

Place the black beans and chickpeas in a container large enough to hold twice the volume. Cover with 3 cups of water and refrigerate for a minimum of 12 hours, although 24 hours is ideal.

Set the machine to sauté and allow it to preheat for 4–5 minutes.

Add the olive oil and allow it to heat up for 30 seconds. Add the turkey, dispersing it evenly into the bottom of the pot. However tempting, don't stir it up for about 4 minutes. This will allow the turkey to caramelize to a nice golden brown on one side.

After the first stir, sauté for an additional 2–3 minutes, stirring frequently to break up the meat into smaller pieces. It's OK to have a few chunky bits.

Add the red onion, carrot, green pepper, garlic, chili powder, salt, cumin, and chili flakes. Season to taste with freshly ground black pepper. Sauté for 3–4 minutes, stirring frequently.

Rinse and drain the soaked beans and chickpeas and add them to the pot. Then add the diced tomatoes, stock, and red lentils, and stir well to combine. Add the sweet potato and zucchini, arranging them evenly over the top of the liquid. Don't stir.

Secure the lid and set the machine for 20 minutes on high pressure, allowing for a 10-minute natural release before completely depressurizing the pot.

Remove the lid, stir well, and serve with green onions, grated Cheddar, and sour cream.

Makes 4 quarts

1 cup dried black beans
½ cup dried chickpeas
2 tbsp olive oil
1 lb ground turkey
1 medium red onion, cut into ¼-inch dice
1 medium carrot, cut into ¼-inch dice
1 medium green bell pepper, cut into ½-inch dice
2 cloves garlic, chopped
1 tbsp chili powder
2 tsp kosher salt
¼ tsp cumin seeds, freshly ground
¼ tsp dried chili flakes
freshly ground black pepper
two 28-oz (796 ml) cans diced tomatoes
2 cups chicken or vegetable stock
½ cup dried red lentils, rinsed and drained
1 medium sweet potato, cut into 1-inch dice
1 medium zucchini, cut into 1-inch dice
3 green onions, chopped
2 cups grated Cheddar cheese
½ cup sour cream

Thai Green Curry Turkey

Move over, chicken breast – turkey's back in town. This aromatic curry is best served with basmati rice (page 98). A cautionary note: it's spicy enough to make your eyelids sweat, and it's meant to be that way. By breaking down a little during the pressure cook, the eggplant helps to thicken the sauce.

Grind together the coriander seeds, cumin seeds, and peppercorns using a mortar and pestle or a spice grinder.

To make the curry paste, place the Thai bird chilies, garlic, shallots, lemongrass, cilantro sprigs, lime zest, and salt in a food processor. Add the ground spice mix and pulse until the paste has a uniform consistency. Set aside until ready to use. (You will have twice as much curry paste as needed for the recipe. Refrigerate the remainder for up to a week or freeze for up to 3 months.)

Place the turkey breast, chicken stock, eggplant, and ½ cup of the green curry paste into the pot and stir well to coat everything in the paste. Add the lime leaves and secure the lid.

Set the machine for 8 minutes on high pressure. Once the pressure cooking cycle has finished, depressurize completely using the quick release method.

Remove the lid and set the machine to sauté. Add the red finger chili and bok choy, and stir for about 1 minute.

Turn off the machine, stir in the coconut cream, Thai basil, and chopped cilantro, and you're ready to serve.

Serves 4–6

Note: It's OK to use coconut milk if you can't get coconut cream.

1 tsp coriander seeds

1 tsp cumin seeds

1 tsp white peppercorns

12 green Thai bird chili peppers, stems removed

8 cloves garlic

2 medium shallots

2 stalks lemongrass, outer layer removed, white parts only

10 sprigs fresh cilantro (stems and leaves attached)

zest of 1 lime

2 tsp kosher salt

1½-lb turkey breast, cut into 1-inch dice

1 cup chicken stock

3 cups Japanese or Sicilian eggplant, cut into 1-inch dice

2 lime leaves

1 long red finger chili, thinly sliced in rings

2 cups bok choy leaves, each leaf cut in half

½ cup coconut cream (see Note)

½ cup chopped fresh Thai basil

½ cup chopped fresh cilantro leaves

Duck Cassoulet

Cassoulet, named for its original cooking vessel, traditionally contained a plethora of meat cuts – generally whatever was on hand at the time. This hearty version has come a long way from its peasant origins. Although there's a lot of pork in it, it is the duck that gives this dish its signature flavour.

Place the white beans into a container large enough to hold double the volume. Cover with 2 cups of water and refrigerate for a minimum of 12 hours, although 24 hours is ideal.

Set the machine to sauté and add the ½ cup of water, the duck fat, and duck legs, skin side down. Sauté for 5–6 minutes, until all the water has boiled off and the duck skin is golden brown. Remove the legs, and add the pancetta and the sausages. Sauté for 4–5 minutes, turning once, until the meat is a nice golden brown. Remove the pancetta and the sausages and set aside.

Add the onion, carrot, celery, leek, and salt. Season to taste with freshly ground pepper, and sauté for 2–3 minutes to lightly soften the vegetables, stirring frequently.

Stir in the white wine and use a wooden spoon to scrape off any bits that may be stuck to the bottom of the pot.

Rinse and drain the soaked beans and add them to the pot, along with the fresh herbs and tomato. Stir in the chicken stock.

Place the pork hock into the pot, submerging it in the liquid. Place the duck legs, pancetta, and sausages on top, and secure the lid.

Set the machine for 35 minutes on high pressure, allowing for a 15-minute natural release before completely depressurizing the pot.

Remove the lid and transfer the meats to a cutting board. Pull the meat off the pork hock, trying not to shred it too fine. Do the same with the duck legs if you wish or serve bone-in. Cut the pancetta and sausages into large pieces and return all the meat to the pot, give everything a stir, and you're ready to serve.

Serves 4

1 cup dried white beans

½ cup water

2 tbsp duck fat

2 duck legs (8 oz each)

two ½-inch-thick slices pancetta

2 fresh sausages, chef's choice

1 medium onion, diced

1 medium carrot, diced

1 stalk celery, diced

1 medium leek, white and light green sections only, halved lengthwise, washed well, and cut into ½-inch slices

2 tsp kosher salt

freshly ground black pepper

½ cup white wine

2 tbsp chopped fresh herbs (such as rosemary, thyme, sage, parsley, and oregano)

1 large tomato, diced

2 cups chicken stock

1 small (1½ lb) smoked pork hock

Everyone's Irish Stew

LAMB

Leg of Lamb with White Wine Gravy

Maybe not for every night, but this boneless leg of lamb, marinated in mustard and garlic, is a treat. You do the work the day before and pop it into the electric pressure cooker when you're ready. Don't rush the resting! It's important to allow for the extra 20 minutes after the pressure cooking cycle ends to allow the meat to finish cooking into the middle.

Some boneless legs of lamb come in a net, giving them a round appearance. You'll want to remove the net before marinating, and then open up the roast to access the entire surface area. The marinade will penetrate the meat much more efficiently. Pay attention to how the leg was rolled up – it will help later when you need to truss it.

In a small bowl, mix together the minced garlic, mustard, olive oil, rosemary, and salt, and season to taste with freshly ground black pepper.

Coat the leg of lamb evenly on all sides with the mustard mixture.

Cut two 18-inch pieces of butcher's twine and place them parallel to each other on your work surface. Place the lamb on top and roll it up as best you can (see photo below). It should at least fold over on itself. Tie tightly with both pieces of twine. Cover and refrigerate for 12–24 hours.

Recipe continues . . .

6–8 cloves garlic, minced

¼ cup Dijon mustard

2 tbsp olive oil

1 tbsp chopped fresh rosemary

1 tbsp kosher salt

freshly ground black pepper

one 4- to 5-lb boneless leg of lamb

1 cup white wine

2–3 tbsp roux (page 19)

2 tbsp chopped fresh parsley

Place the white wine in the pot and then put in the trivet. Place the lamb on the trivet and pour in any excess marinade. Secure the lid, and set the machine for 35 minutes on high pressure.

Once the pressure cooking cycle has finished, depressurize completely using the quick release method. Do not remove the lid.

Allow to rest for 20 minutes (machine off) with the lid on.

Remove the lid and carefully remove the lamb roast from the pot. Transfer to a cutting board for carving. Remove the trivet from the pot.

Set the machine to sauté and bring the juices to a boil. Turn off the machine.

Make the gravy by immediately whisking in the roux, half a tablespoon at a time, until the desired consistency is reached. Remember that the sauce will continue to thicken as it cools. Stir in the parsley.

Cut the strings off the roast and slice the lamb against the grain as best as possible. (The grain will change directions as you go because of the different muscles that make up the leg.) You'll have a crowd-pleasing variety of slices, ranging from medium rare to well done. Serve with the white wine gravy.

Serves 6–8

Everyone's Irish Stew

They say everyone's a little Irish at least once a year. Here's your chance to be Irish as often as you'd like. The simplicity shines through in this recipe like a pot of gold, allowing for deliciously clean flavours.

Set the machine to sauté and add the butter, carrots, celery, onion, potatoes, thyme, and salt. Season to taste with freshly ground black pepper. Sauté for 5 minutes, stirring frequently.

Stir in the lamb and lamb stock, and secure the lid.

Set the machine for 20 minutes on high pressure. Allow for a 15-minute natural release before completely depressurizing the pot.

Remove the lid, stir in the parsley, and spoon the stew into bowls.

Serve with crusty bread and salted butter.

Serves 4–6

Note: If you can't find boneless lamb shoulder, ask your butcher to debone one for you, and keep the bones to make stock for this recipe.

2 tbsp butter

2 large carrots, roughly cut into 1-inch pieces

2 large stalks celery, roughly cut into 1-inch pieces

1 large sweet onion, cut into 1-inch dice

4–5 medium Yukon gold potatoes, quartered (4 cups)

1 tbsp roughly chopped fresh thyme

2 tsp kosher salt

freshly ground black pepper

1½- to 2-lb boneless lamb shoulder, cut into 1-inch dice (see Note)

2 cups lamb stock (or substitute chicken stock)

¼ cup chopped fresh parsley

Moroccan Spiced Lamb

Historically, this dish would be cooked slowly in an earthenware pot called a tagine. The electric pressure cooker speeds things up immensely. Make a quick batch of couscous to round out the meal.

Place the dried chickpeas into a container large enough to hold double the volume. Cover with 2 cups of water and refrigerate for a minimum of 12 hours, although 24 hours is ideal.

Set the machine to sauté and add the coriander seeds, cumin seeds, fennel seeds, peppercorns, chili flakes, and cinnamon. Stir frequently for 3-4 minutes to toast the spices, drawing their flavours to the forefront. Remove the spices and set aside to cool slightly before grinding them in a mortar and pestle or spice grinder. (You'll need only 2 tbsp of the Moroccan spice mixture for this recipe, so store the balance in an airtight container for use in future recipes.)

Season the lamb with 2 tablespoons of the Moroccan spice mixture and the salt.

Set the machine to sauté and allow it to preheat for 4–5 minutes.

Add the olive oil and the seasoned lamb, dispersing it evenly in the bottom of the pot. However tempting, don't stir up the meat for about 5 minutes. This will allow the lamb to caramelize to a nice golden brown on one side. You may want to do this step in batches to avoid overcrowding the pot.

Once the lamb is browned and removed from the pot, add the apricots, tomatoes, onion, lemon zest, almonds, and ginger. Continue to sauté for 5 minutes, stirring frequently.

Add the stock, passata, and seared lamb. Add the soaked, drained, and rinsed chickpeas and stir well. Bring to a simmer before you secure the lid.

Secure the lid and set the machine for 20 minutes on high pressure. Allow for a 15-minute natural release before completely depressurizing the pot.

Remove the lid and serve lamb with couscous.

Serves 4–8

1 cup dried chickpeas

6 tbsp coriander seeds

2 tbsp cumin seeds

1 tbsp fennel seeds

½ tbsp black peppercorns

½ tsp chili flakes

½ small cinnamon stick, broken
   into small pieces

1½- to 2-lb boneless lamb
   shoulder, cut into 1-inch dice

2 tsp kosher salt

2 tbsp olive oil

12 dried apricots, diced
   (about ½ cup)

2 plum tomatoes, diced

1 large onion, diced

zest of 1 lemon

¼ cup sliced almonds

2 tbsp minced fresh ginger

2 cups chicken stock
   (lamb stock if you have it)

¾ cup passata

Garam Masala Lamb

Garam masala is a blend of ground spices common in Indian and South Asian cuisines. Using a bone-in cut of lamb will add a stronger lamb flavour to the dish, and that's exactly what's needed to stand up to the freshly toasted spices. In the event of leftovers, pull the bones out, mix together the meat, potatoes, and lentils, and you have the perfect filling for roti or flour tortillas.

Set the machine to sauté. Make the garam masala by adding the cinnamon, cumin seeds, coriander seeds, peppercorns, fennel seeds, allspice, cardamom seeds, and cloves. Stir frequently for 3-4 minutes to toast the spices, drawing their flavours to the forefront. Remove the spices and set aside to cool slightly before grinding them in a mortar and pestle or spice grinder. You'll need only 2 tbsp for this recipe, so store the balance in an airtight container for use in future recipes.

Mix together 2 tbsp garam masala, garlic, green onions, yogurt, turmeric, Thai bird chili, and 2 tsp of salt.

Marinate the lamb in this mixture and refrigerate for at least 1 hour or overnight.

Set the machine to sauté and add the ghee, onion, and 1 tsp of salt. Sauté, stirring frequently, for 4–5 minutes to brown the onion a little.

Add the chicken stock, lentils, potatoes, and marinated lamb. Add any excess marinade to the pot as well.

Secure the lid and set the machine for 15 minutes on high pressure, allowing for a 10-minute natural release before completely depressurizing the pot.

Remove the lid and the lamb is ready to serve.

Serves 4

For the garam masala:

1 small cinnamon stick, broken into small pieces

1½ tbsp cumin seeds

2 tsp coriander seeds

2 tsp black peppercorns

1 tsp fennel seeds

1 tsp whole allspice

½ tsp cardamom seeds (the part inside the pods)

½ tsp whole cloves

For the lamb:

3 cloves garlic, minced

3 green onions, minced

½ cup plain full-fat yogurt

1 tbsp turmeric

1 green Thai bird chili, minced

2 tsp kosher salt

four ½-lb lamb shoulder chops, ½–¾ inches thick

2 tbsp ghee

1 medium onion, finely diced

1 tsp kosher salt

4 cups chicken stock

2 cups dried red lentils, rinsed and drained

2–3 medium potatoes, cut into 1-inch dice (about 2 cups)

Simple Steamed Mussels

FISH AND SEAFOOD

Jumbo Shrimp Cocktail

This is an incredibly efficient way to cook shrimp for a party or special family meal (but make sure you have a metal steamer basket handy). You'll never again buy a shrimp ring once you've tried these big, plump crustaceans cooked under pressure for only a minute. Serve with spiced ketchup (page 33) for dipping.

In a large bowl, toss together the shrimp, white wine, salt, and hot sauce.

Pour the water into the pot, then place a stainless-steel steamer basket inside.

Place the shrimp evenly into the basket, allowing for minimal overlap. Secure the lid and set the machine for 1 minute on high pressure.

Depressurize completely using the quick release method and remove the lid.

Transfer the shrimp to a plate and cover with a cool, damp paper towel. Set aside to cool a little before putting the shrimp in the fridge to cool completely.

Peel, dip, and eat when ready!

Serves 4–6

Notes: Buy frozen shrimp and thaw them in the fridge overnight for best results. Many grocery stores with a fresh fish counter merely thaw frozen shrimp, and customers may assume they're fresh. Buying direct from the freezer allows you more control over how long the shrimp are in their thawed state and therefore how fresh they will taste.

16/20 refers to the size of the shrimp. It means that there are 16–20 shrimp per pound. Shrimp are also sold 21/25, but they are smaller, needing 21–25 shrimp to make up a pound.

twelve 16/20 count shrimp, shell on (see Notes)

1 tbsp white wine

1 tsp kosher salt

hot sauce to taste

1 cup water

Jambalaya

Cajun or Creole? It's hard to trace the origins of some dishes because the cuisine in Louisiana overlaps the two cultures. To oversimplify matters, Creole cuisine uses tomato as a main ingredient, and Cajun cuisine does not, making this recipe land on the Creole side. It starts with the "holy trinity" of vegetables – onion, celery, and green pepper – which is the Louisiana version of *mirepoix*.

Set the machine to sauté and allow it to preheat for 4–5 minutes. Add the peanut oil and use a wooden spoon or heat-resistant spatula to make sure the oil has coated the bottom of the pot.

Add the onions, green peppers, celery, garlic, and salt, and sauté, stirring frequently, for 7–8 minutes, until the vegetables are soft and starting to brown. Add the thyme, paprika, tomato paste, and roux, and stir well for 1 minute.

Add the chicken and okra, followed by the tomatoes, chicken stock, rice, and bay leaf, and stir well. Float the Scotch bonnet pepper on top and secure the lid.

Set the machine for 10 minutes on high pressure. Allow for a 5-minute natural release before completely depressurizing the pot.

Remove the lid and set the machine to sauté. Once the jambalaya is simmering, stir in the snapper, shrimp, and cilantro.

Turn off the machine. Place the lid back on the machine and allow to sit for 5 minutes – the residual heat will cook the shrimp and snapper. The machine should remain off during the 5 minutes.

Remove the lid, stir, and serve.

Serves 6–8

Note: The Scotch bonnet pepper should be intact when you remove the lid. Check the spice level of the jambalaya. If you want more heat, chop the pepper and return some or all of it to the pot.

2 tbsp peanut oil

2 medium onions, diced

1 large green bell pepper, diced

2 stalks celery, diced

3 cloves garlic, thinly sliced

1 tbsp kosher salt

2 tbsp chopped fresh thyme

1 tbsp paprika

1 tbsp tomato paste

2 tbsp roux (page 19)

1 lb chicken thighs, boneless and skinless, each cut into 6–8 pieces

2 cups sliced okra (¼-inch slices)

one 28-oz (796 ml) can diced tomatoes

4 cups chicken stock

⅓ cup long-grain white rice

1 bay leaf

1 Scotch bonnet pepper, whole (see Note)

½ lb red snapper filets, boneless, cut into 1-inch square pieces

½ lb 16/20 count shrimp, peeled, deveined, and each cut into 3–4 pieces

½ cup chopped fresh cilantro

Chicken, Grouper, and Chorizo Paella

There's no wrong way to make this one, as long as there's rice, saffron, and olive oil. Paella is a Spanish classic originating in Valencia, and it gets its name from the Latin word *patella*, meaning "pan." Traditionally cooked over an open fire in a larger-than-life frying pan.

Set the machine to sauté and allow it to preheat for 4–5 minutes.

Add the olive oil and use a wooden spoon or heat-resistant spatula to make sure the oil has coated the bottom of the pot.

Add the chorizo, dispersing it evenly into the bottom of the pot in small chunks. However tempting, don't stir it up for about 4–5 minutes. This will allow the sausage to caramelize to a nice golden brown on one side.

After the first stir, sauté for an additional 1–2 minutes, stirring frequently to further break up the meat.

Add the red onion, red pepper, celery, tomato paste, and salt. Cook, stirring frequently, for 3–4 minutes or until the vegetables are softened but not yet browning.

Stir in the rice and add the stock, bay leaf, and saffron.

Stir in the chicken and the grouper, and secure the lid.

Set the machine for 6 minutes on high pressure. Once the pressure cooking cycle has finished, depressurize completely using the quick release method.

Remove the lid and stir in the green onions and fresh tomatoes.

Serves 4–6

Notes: Saffron has a distinct flavour that dissipates quicker than some of the other things in your spice cabinet. For best results, commit to making a few dishes with saffron and use it up within a year.

The grouper can be replaced with many types of firm-fleshed white fish, such as mahi mahi, swordfish, snapper, or kingfish.

- ½ tbsp olive oil
- 8 oz chorizo sausage, casings removed
- 1 small red onion, diced
- ½ red bell pepper, diced
- 1 stalk celery, diced
- 1 tbsp tomato paste
- 2 tsp kosher salt
- ¾ cup converted rice, rinsed and drained
- 1 cup chicken or vegetable stock
- 1 bay leaf
- 15–20 strands (a pinch or two) saffron (see Note)
- 8 oz chicken thighs, boneless and skinless, cut into 1-inch cubes
- 8 oz grouper, boneless and skinless, cut into 1- to 2-inch cubes (see Note)
- 2 green onions, finely sliced
- 2 plum tomatoes, seeds removed, cut into ¼-inch dice

One-Pot Salmon Dinner

A well-rounded meal for two people. Everything goes into the pressure cooker at once: honey mustard and white wine–marinated salmon with fresh asparagus and quinoa. A glass of chardonnay might be in order.

Grease a 6-inch round cake pan (3 inches deep) with butter or cooking spray.

Arrange the asparagus pieces evenly in the bottom of the pan. Arrange the salmon filets evenly on top of the asparagus.

In a small bowl, stir together the white wine, whole-grain mustard, honey, ½ tsp of salt, and pepper to taste. Spoon the sauce over the top of each piece of salmon.

Set the machine to sauté and add the butter, shallot, and 1 tsp of salt, and sauté for 2 minutes, stirring frequently.

Add the quinoa and 1 cup + 2 tbsp of water, and stir.

Turn off the sauté function and place the trivet in the pot. Place the cake pan (with the salmon and asparagus in it) onto the trivet. Secure the lid.

Set the machine for 2 minutes on high pressure, allowing for a 5-minute natural release before completely depressurizing the pot.

Remove the pan of salmon and remove the trivet.

Fluff the quinoa with a wooden spoon.

Serve with lemon wedges and, perhaps, a nice white wine. Each serving should include quinoa, asparagus, and salmon, topped with the juices from the cake pan.

Serves 2

10–12 spears asparagus, sliced into 2-inch pieces (about 2 cups)

two 6-oz salmon filets

3 tbsp white wine

2 tbsp whole-grain mustard

1 tsp honey

½ tsp kosher salt

freshly ground black pepper

1 tbsp butter

1 shallot, thinly sliced

1 tsp kosher salt

1 cup quinoa, rinsed and drained

1 cup + 2 tbsp water

1 lemon, cut into wedges

Cioppino

Italians who settled in the San Francisco Bay area used the familiarity of a saltwater coast to carry on the tradition of making a bistro-style "catch-of-the-day" soup using up whatever the fishermen brought ashore. Once you get the hang of this recipe, try substituting different seafood, such as halibut or mahi mahi.

Set the machine to sauté. Add the olive oil, onion, fennel, leek, thyme, and serrano pepper, and sauté for 7–8 minutes or until the vegetables are softened and just starting to brown.

Add the tomato paste and stir well for 1 minute.

Add the vermouth and stir well for about 1 minute.

Add the diced tomatoes and the water and bring to a boil, stirring frequently.

Add the clams and red snapper, and secure the lid.

Set the machine to 3 minutes on high pressure. Once the pressure cooking cycle has finished, depressurize completely using the quick release method.

Remove the lid and add the shrimp, scallops, basil, and salt, stirring them into the soup.

Place the lid back on the machine and allow to sit for 2 minutes, allowing the residual heat to cook the shrimp and scallops. The machine should remain off during the 2 minutes.

Remove the lid and season to taste with freshly ground black pepper. Serve with fresh crusty bread for sopping up the tasty juices.

Serves 4–6

Notes: Littleneck clams are small and are sometimes called pasta clams.

U15 refers to the size of the scallop, meaning under 15 scallops per pound. These are pretty big ones!

1 tbsp olive oil

1 medium onion, diced

½ bulb fennel, diced

1 small leek, white and light green sections only, halved lengthwise, washed well, and diced

1 tbsp chopped fresh thyme

1 serrano pepper, minced

1 tbsp tomato paste

2 oz dry vermouth

one 28-oz (796 ml) can diced tomatoes

1 cup water

1½ lb (about 25 pieces) fresh littleneck clams, washed well to remove surface grit (see Note)

1 lb fresh red snapper, large dice

twelve 16/20 count shrimp, peeled and deveined, each cut into 3–4 pieces

½ lb (about 7) U15 count scallops, cut into ¼-inch slices (see Note)

2 tbsp chopped fresh basil

1 tsp kosher salt

freshly ground black pepper

Simple Steamed Mussels

Try this version first to get the hang of things – and then have some fun. Add leeks, garlic, lemon zest, cream, fresh tomato, and on and on. Always great with good bread and your favourite wine or beer.

Set the machine to sauté and add the butter, shallots, thyme, salt, and freshly ground black pepper, and sauté for 3 minutes, stirring frequently.

Add the wine and stir for 20 to 30 seconds.

Add the mussels and secure the lid.

Set the machine for 1 minute on high pressure. Once the pressure cooking cycle has finished, depressurize completely using the quick release method.

Remove the lid and spoon the mussels into a large bowl, with the shallots and juices.

Serve with lemon wedges, crusty bread, and lots of napkins.

Serves 4–6

Notes: This recipe is easily halved. Use the full ½ cup of wine when halving the recipe.

You can substitute water for some or all of the wine. Alternatively, use a mild- to medium-bodied beer instead.

3 tbsp butter

3 medium shallots, thinly sliced

3 sprigs fresh thyme

½ tsp kosher salt

½ tsp freshly ground black pepper

½ cup white wine (see Note)

4–5 lb mussels, washed, beards removed

1 lemon, cut into wedges

1 loaf crusty bread

East Coast Clam Boil

Bring the beach inside with this old-time East Coast delight. In this boil, sometimes called a steamer pot, layers of meat, vegetables, and seafood are cooked together. It's the epitome of a one-pot meal. Get the melted butter ready and grab a bib. This one can get a little messy, and that's part of the fun.

Pour the beer and water into the pot and add the bay leaves.

In a large bowl, toss together the potatoes, corn, and shrimp with the thyme, salt, and paprika. Place the corn and potatoes into the pot. Next place the pieces of sausage on top, followed by the shrimp. Place the clams on last and secure the lid.

Set the machine for 5 minutes on high pressure. Once the pressure cooking cycle has finished, depressurize completely using the quick release method.

Remove the lid and divide the contents into bowls. Serve with freshly ground black pepper, lots of melted butter on the side, and lemon wedges.

Serves 4

Notes: You can use a multitude of different sausages for this recipe, from a mild Italian to the spiciest chorizo. Choose the right one for your crowd.

There are many versions of this recipe. Additions range from onions and garlic to mussels and lobster tails.

½ cup light-bodied beer
¼ cup water
2 bay leaves
4 medium red potatoes, each cut into 6–8 wedges
2 cobs corn, husks removed, each cut into 4 rounds
twelve 16/20 count shrimp, shells on
2 tbsp chopped fresh thyme
1 tsp kosher salt
1 tsp paprika
two 4–5-oz sausages (chef's choice), cut in half (see Note)
25 (1½ lb) littleneck clams, washed well to remove surface grit
freshly ground black pepper
melted butter
1 lemon, cut into wedges

Chai Spice Poached Pear

Rice Pudding

Rice pudding is a dessert – sometimes a breakfast, too – for all walks of life and is popular around the world. It's delicious as is, but feel free to top it with peaches, bananas, berries, or other fresh fruit.

Set the machine to sauté and add the milk, sugar, salt, and cinnamon to the pot. Bring the milk to a simmer, stirring frequently to prevent scorching.

Add the rice, stir, and secure the lid.

Set the machine for 10 minutes on high pressure, allowing for a 10-minute natural release before completely depressurizing the pot.

Remove the lid and set the machine to sauté.

Scoop about ½ cup of rice into a small bowl and whisk in the eggs. Stir this mixture into the rest of the rice in the pot and cook for 1–2 minutes until it thickens. Turn off the machine.

Stir in the currants. You now have a delicious pressure cooker rice pudding that can be served warm or cold.

Makes 4½ cups

3 cups 2% milk

⅓ cup sugar

pinch kosher salt

pinch ground cinnamon

½ cup arborio rice

2 eggs, whisked together

¼ cup currants

Fruit-Bottom Cheesecake Cups

Traditional oven-baked cheesecake requires you to work a little – whisking air into the batter to create the desired texture. With the electric pressure cooker, you skip this step. Too much air in the batter is, in fact, your enemy because it will cause the cheesecake to expand too fast under pressure and probably make a mess in your machine. So use a whisk to fold in the ingredients, not whip them. You'll need four 8-oz wide-mouth canning jars with lids for this recipe.

Place the cream cheese into a large bowl and cream it using a sturdy whisk.

Fold in the sugar, cornstarch, and salt until fully incorporated.

Fold in the egg and vanilla until fully incorporated.

Fold in the sour cream and the lemon juice.

Place 1 tbsp of blueberry compote into each of the 4 canning jars, reserving the rest for the tops once ready to serve.

Divide the cheesecake batter equally among the jars. Loosely screw on the lids, tightening just enough so they stay in place but air can escape.

Place the trivet in the pot and add the water for steaming.

Carefully set the lidded jars onto the trivet. Secure the pressure cooker lid and set the machine for 10 minutes on high pressure, allowing for a 15-minute natural release before completely depressurizing the pot.

Remove the pressure cooker lid and allow the jars to cool slightly before carefully removing them with canning tongs. Carefully remove the lids right away. (You may need gloves or a kitchen towel – they're hot!)

Once the cheesecakes have cooled to room temperature, serve garnished with the remaining blueberry compote. If you like your cheesecake cold, refrigerate before serving.

Serves 4

Note: Inspect your jars regularly for cracks. Slightly cracked jars will not survive the rigours of a pressure cook cycle.

1 lb cream cheese, softened

⅔ cup sugar

2 tbsp cornstarch

¼ tsp kosher salt

1 large egg

2 tsp vanilla extract

½ cup sour cream

¼ lemon, juiced (1 tbsp)

½ cup blueberry compote (page 265)

1 cup water, for steaming

Pots de Crème

These little gems invite many toppings, from whipped cream and chocolate shavings to caramel and berries. The EPC is initially used as a double boiler. You'll need six 4-oz wide-mouth canning jars with lids and a stainless steel bowl big enough to sit on – not in – the lidless pot.

Place the water into the pot, set to sauté, and bring it to a boil. Place the chocolate in a metal bowl and set on top of the lidless pot. Allow the chocolate to melt but not overcook, 3–5 minutes. Turn off the machine and leave the bowl sitting over the hot water.

In a large bowl, whisk together the cream and milk, and very slowly add half of this mixture to the chocolate, whisking constantly. Then add the other half all at once and whisk to combine.

Remove the bowl from the top of the pot. Take care to ensure that the bowl is not suctioned to the pot. A little wiggle should break the seal. Leave the water in the pot for the pressure cooking cycle.

Add the sugar and whisk well to combine. Add the egg yolks and whisk until smooth.

Pour the mixture evenly into 6 canning jars. Loosely screw on the lids, tightening just enough so they stay in place but air can still escape.

Place the trivet into the bottom of the pot. Place the lidded jars onto the trivet, 5 around the edge and 1 in the middle. Secure the pressure cooker lid and set the machine for 4 minutes on high pressure, allowing for a 10-minute natural release before completely depressurizing the pot.

Remove the pressure cooker lid and carefully remove the jars from the pot with canning tongs. Remove the lids right away. (You may need gloves or a kitchen towel - they're hot!) Set jars aside to cool on a rack for about half an hour. Refrigerate for at least 2 hours before serving. Garnish at will.

Serves 6

Note: Inspect your jars regularly for cracks. Slightly cracked jars will not survive the rigours of a pressure cook cycle.

1½ cups water, for double boiler

3½ oz semisweet chocolate chips/chopped-up chocolate bar

1¼ cups 35% cream

¼ cup 2% milk

3 tbsp sugar

3 egg yolks

Salted Crème de Dulce de Leche

This dessert, based on a classic crème brûlée, is the only recipe in the book that specifically calls for sea salt. Maldon brand sea salt is harvested to produce soft, crunchy flakes that are unexpectedly not too salty. You'll need six 4-oz wide-mouth canning jars with lids for this recipe.

Whisk together the egg, egg yolks, and dulce de leche until the mixture has a uniform consistency. Whisk in the cream, vanilla, and salt. Pass through a fine sieve.

Divide the batter evenly into 6 canning jars. Loosely screw on the lids, tightening just enough so they stay in place but air can still escape.

Pour the water for steaming into the pot. Place the trivet in the pot and carefully set the lidded jars evenly onto it. You should fit 5 around the edge and 1 in the middle.

Secure the pressure cooker lid and set the machine for 3 minutes on high pressure, allowing for a 15-minute natural release before completely depressurizing the pot.

Remove the pressure cooker lid, allow to cool slightly, and remove each jar using canning tongs. Carefully remove the lids right away. (You may need gloves or a kitchen towel – they're hot!)

Allow the jars to cool to room temperature before placing them in the refrigerator for at least 2 hours before serving. Serve cold, garnished with a small spoonful of dulce de leche and a pinch of sea salt on top of each portion.

Serves 6

Note: Inspect your jars regularly for cracks. Slightly cracked jars will not survive the rigours of a pressure cook cycle.

1 large egg

2 egg yolks

½ cup dulce de leche (page 267) at room temperature

1¼ cups 35% cream

1 tsp vanilla extract

¼ tsp sea salt

1½ cups water, for steaming

2 tbsp dulce de leche for garnishing

sea salt for garnishing

Chai Spice Poached Pear

Poached pears have been around since Shakespeare's day, and rightly so. These tender, tasty treats are no longer just for fancy dinners. They're so easy in the electric pressure cooker that you'll prepare them all the time. Bosc or Bartlett pears are best for this recipe because of their firmness.

Place all ingredients, expect for the pears, into the pot. Set the machine to sauté. Bring the mixture to a simmer, stirring frequently.

Turn off the machine and allow the mixture to steep for 15 minutes.

Strain the leaves and spices from the liquid into a small bowl. Return the flavoured syrup to the pot, discarding the leaves and spices. Add the pears and secure the lid.

Set the machine for 6 minutes on high pressure. Once the pressure cooking cycle has finished, depressurize completely using the quick release method.

Remove the pressure cooker lid and allow the pears to cool slightly in the syrup. Keep the pears in the syrup until you're ready to serve them.

Serve warm with ice cream.

Serves 4–8

Notes: Put the tea leaves and spices into a do-it-yourself tea bag for easy removal.

A melon baller is great for removing the pear cores.

Handle the pears gently once they're cooked since they'll be soft, making them susceptible to cuts and bruises.

10 cardamom pods

4 cloves

2 peeled fresh ginger coins, ¼-inch thick

2 cups water

1 small cinnamon stick

½ lime, juiced (1½ tbsp)

½ cup sugar

2 tsp Earl Grey tea leaves (see Note)

½ tsp black peppercorns

¼ tsp fennel seeds

¼ vanilla bean, scraped (use the scraped seeds)

4 pears, peeled, cut in half, cores scooped out (see Note)

Banana Marshmallow Sticky Cakes

This twist on banana bread is best served warm. Not to worry. The kids will probably gobble up the cakes before they have a chance to cool. You'll need six 4-oz wide-mouth canning jars with lids for this recipe.

Prepare the 6 canning jars by coating the inside surfaces with non-stick cooking spray.

In a bowl, mash up the bananas with a fork and add the egg, flour, ½ cup mini-marshmallows, brown sugar, melted butter, maple syrup, chocolate chips, cocoa powder, baking powder, vanilla, salt, and cinnamon. Mix everything together with the fork.

Spoon this mixture evenly into the jars. Loosely screw the lids on the jars, tightening just enough so they stay in place but air can still escape.

Place the trivet in the pot and add the water for steaming. Set the jars onto the trivet. You should fit 5 around the edge and 1 in the middle.

Secure the lid and set the machine for 6 minutes on high pressure, allowing for a 10-minute natural release before completely depressurizing the pot.

Remove the pressure cooker lid. Carefully lift the jars from the trivet using canning tongs and remove the lids from the jars. (You will need gloves or a kitchen towel – they're hot!)

While the cakes are still warm, divide the remaining ½ cup of marshmallows among the tops.

Serves 6

Notes: Inspect your jars regularly for cracks. Slightly cracked jars will not survive the rigours of a pressure cook cycle.

Why garnish with marshmallows alone? Add some extra chocolate chips and banana slices to take your cakes to the next level.

2 very ripe bananas, peeled

1 large egg

½ cup all-purpose flour

½ cup mini-marshmallows

½ cup dark brown sugar

¼ cup butter, melted

¼ cup maple syrup

¼ cup semisweet chocolate chips

2 tbsp cocoa powder

½ tsp baking powder

½ tsp vanilla extract

pinch kosher salt

pinch ground cinnamon

1½ cups water, for steaming

½ cup mini-marshmallows (see Note)

Spiced Rhubarb Upside-Down Cake

Self-saucing? Yes, the brown-sugared rhubarb releases liquid as it cooks and combines with the maple syrup to create a sauce beneath the cake. Meanwhile, the cake bakes on top. When you turn it onto a plate, you'll find a cake draped in a deliciously sweet sauce. A great presentation, sure to wow family and guests. You'll need four 4-oz ramekins for this recipe.

Rub the 2 tsp of butter inside the four ½-cup ramekins, coating the bottoms and edges. Place ½ tbsp of sugar into each ramekin and shake it around to coat the buttered surfaces, including the sides. Discard any sugar not stuck to the butter.

In a bowl, mix together the rhubarb and 2 tbsp brown sugar. Divide evenly into the ramekins and add 1 tbsp of maple syrup to each.

In a bowl, whisk together the ¼ cup of butter, ¼ cup of brown sugar, cinnamon, ginger, and vanilla. Whisk in the egg and the molasses.

Mix together the flour and baking powder and fold them into the wet ingredients using a rubber spatula, being careful not to overmix. Divide the batter evenly into each ramekin. Don't stir things up.

Pour the water for steaming into the pot. Place the trivet in the pot and carefully set the filled ramekins onto it, evenly spaced.

Secure the lid and set the machine for 10 minutes on high pressure, allowing for a 10-minute natural release before completely depressurizing the pot.

Remove the lid and then remove each ramekin using canning tongs. Allow to cool sufficiently so you can easily handle the ramekins.

Turn the cakes out onto plates and serve warm, maybe with a little ice cream for the fun of it.

Serves 4

Note: For a festive fall dessert, this recipe works with cranberries in place of rhubarb.

2 tsp butter
2 tbsp sugar
1 cup diced rhubarb (¼-inch dice) (see Note)
2 tbsp light brown sugar
¼ cup maple syrup
¼ cup butter, softened
¼ cup light brown sugar
½ tsp ground cinnamon
½ tsp ground ginger
¼ tsp vanilla extract
1 large egg
2 tbsp fancy molasses
½ cup all-purpose flour
1 tsp baking powder
1½ cups water, for steaming

Carrot Cake with Cream Cheese Icing

Who'd think to make a whole cake in the pressure cooker? It sounds a little crazy, but it works – and it works well. Coating the cake pan in breadcrumbs adds a nice look and lovely texture to the cake. It also helps the cake pop out of the pan easily once cooked. Use non-stick cooking spray for best results.

Prepare a 6-inch round cake pan (3 inches deep) by spraying the inner surface areas with non-stick cooking spray. Add the bread crumbs. Shake and manoeuvre the bread crumbs so they stick to the sprayed surface. Discard unstuck crumbs.

In a large bowl, mix together the flour, almonds, icing sugar, baking powder, cardamom, salt, and orange zest. Add the grated carrots and mix well.

Using a hand mixer or stand mixer, whisk the eggs and sugar until the mixture doubles in volume and is creamy and pale. Using a rubber spatula, fold in the carrot-flour mixture. Fold in the melted butter and pour the mixture into the prepared cake pan.

Place the trivet in the pot and add the water for steaming. Place the uncovered cake pan into the pot, on the trivet, and secure the lid.

Set the machine for 25 minutes on high pressure, allowing for a 10-minute natural release before completely depressurizing the pot.

Remove the lid and carefully remove the cake. Allow the cake to cook for 10 minutes and remove it from the pan by flipping it onto a plate. Flip it over again so it's right-side up. Allow to cool to room temperature before icing.

For the icing, place the cream cheese, butter, and vanilla in a bowl. Using a hand mixer, mix 2–3 minutes for a uniform consistency. Add the icing sugar a ¼ cup at a time, mixing to a uniform consistency after each addition.

Spread the icing over the cake and serve.

Serves 4–6

Note: If you want room temperature eggs in a hurry, place them in a bowl of warm water for about 10 minutes.

3 tbsp dry plain bread crumbs

½ cup all-purpose flour

½ cup ground almonds

¼ cup icing sugar

1 tsp baking powder

¼ tsp ground cardamom

¼ tsp kosher salt

zest of 1 orange

1 cup grated carrot

2 eggs at room temperature (see Note)

¼ cup sugar

¼ cup butter, melted

1½ cups water, for steaming

For the icing:

¼ cup cream cheese, softened

2 tbsp butter, softened

1 tsp vanilla extract

1 cup icing sugar

Strawberry Jam

BREAKFAST AND PRESERVES

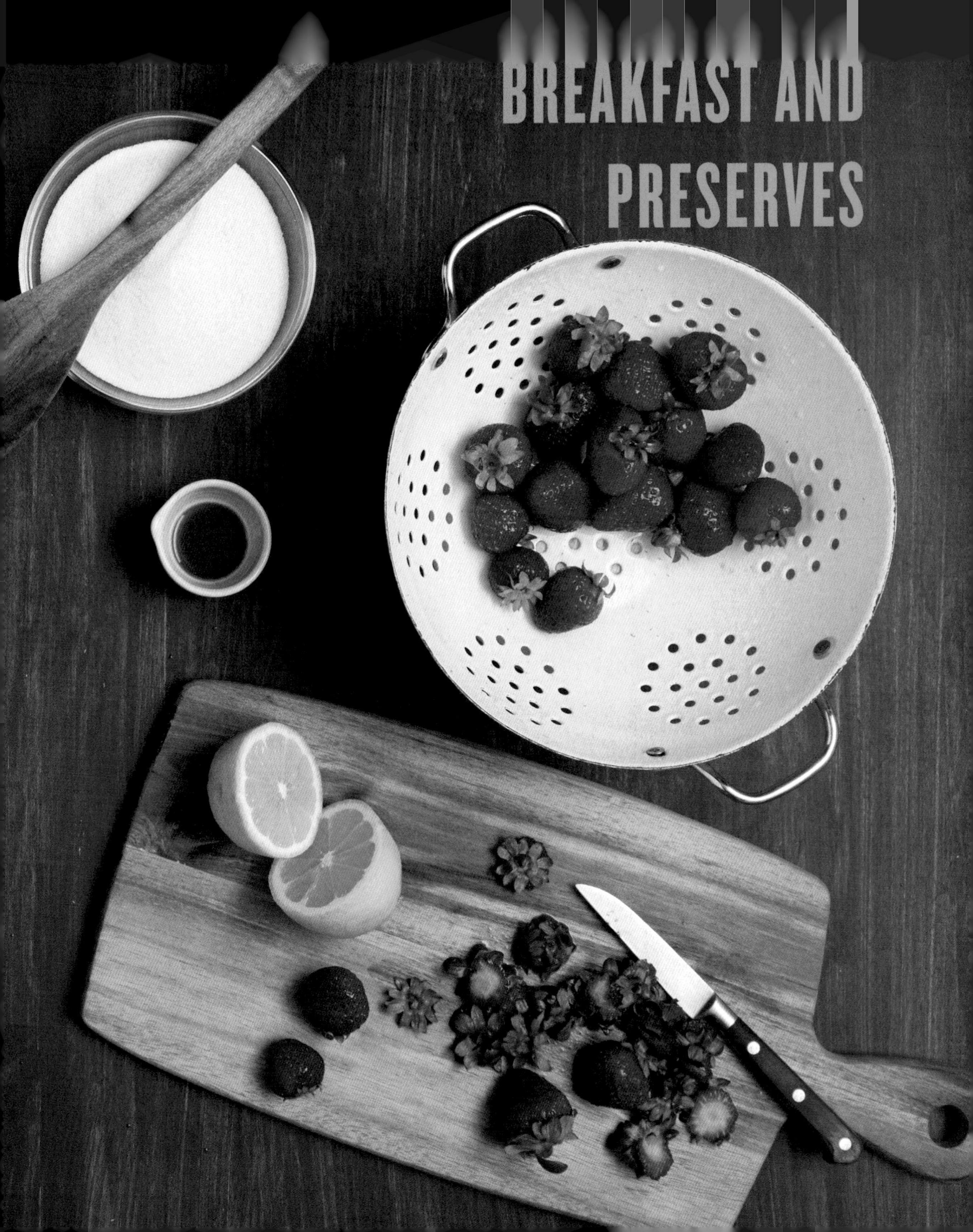

Steel Cut Oats

Steel Cut Oats

Getting the kids to 6 a.m. hockey practice has never been easier. The electric pressure cooker takes care of breakfast – no scorching, no boiling over – while you get yourself caffeinated. Dress up this oatmeal with some applesauce (page 266) and a little maple syrup to give them the power they need to perform.

In the pot, stir together the oats, the water, milk, butter, and salt. Secure the lid.

Set the machine for 5 minutes on high pressure, allowing for a 15-minute natural release before completely depressurizing the pot.

Remove the lid, stir, and serve with a drizzle of honey and a pinch of cinnamon.

Serves 4

Note: This recipe can be easily halved.

2 cups steel cut oats

3 cups water

3 cups 2% milk

¼ cup butter, cut into ½-inch cubes

½ tsp kosher salt

honey

cinnamon

Oatmeal

Here's a comforting breakfast, ready-quick in the electric pressure cooker with minimal effort. Jazz up your oatmeal with fresh fruit for a fast, balanced breakfast. Rolled oats are the same grain as the steel cut variety, but they've been parboiled and rolled flat (squished) to encourage a shorter cooking time.

In the pot, stir together the oats, the water, milk, butter, and salt. Secure the lid.

Set the machine for 2 minutes on high pressure, allowing for a 10-minute natural release before completely depressurizing the pot.

Remove the lid, stir, and serve with a drizzle of honey and a pinch of cinnamon.

Serves 4

Note: This recipe can be easily halved.

2 cups rolled oats

3 cups water

3 cups 2% milk

¼ cup butter, cut into ½-inch cubes

½ tsp kosher salt

honey

cinnamon

Breakfast Strata Jars

For those on the run, an easy breakfast that's easy to put together when you're still half-asleep. Just pop the jars into the electric pressure cooker while you get ready for your day. It's basically a breakfast sandwich in a jar. You'll need two 8-oz wide-mouth canning jars for this recipe.

In a large bowl, whisk together the eggs, milk, and salt. Season to taste with freshly ground black pepper. Add the bread, ham, Cheddar, and chives, and mix together gently.

Grease 2 canning jars with butter or a non-stick cooking spray. Divide the egg mixture evenly into the jars. Loosely screw on the lids, tightening just enough so they stay in place but air can still escape.

Pour the water for steaming into the pot and add the trivet. Place the jars on the trivet, taking care they're not touching each other or the edge of the pot.

Secure the lid and set the machine for 5 minutes on high pressure. Allow for a 15-minute natural release before completely depressurizing the pot. (Your machine may indicate that it's completely depressurized before 15 minutes is up, but do not remove the lid until 15 minutes have passed.)

Remove the pressure cooker lid and allow the jars to sit for 5 minutes so they'll be cool enough to handle. Then remove the jars with canning tongs.

Remove the lids and dig in.

Serves 2

Notes: Inspect your jars regularly for cracks. Slightly cracked jars will not survive the rigours of a pressure cook cycle.

You can play with the ingredients a little. For example, for the ham, substitute other cooked meats that you find in the fridge. Just don't add anything too high in moisture, such as raw vegetables.

Throw a proper lid on the jar and take it on the road with you.

3 large eggs

2 tbsp 2% milk

½ tsp kosher salt

freshly ground black pepper

½ cup diced bread

½ cup diced ham (see Note)

½ cup grated Cheddar cheese

1 tbsp chopped fresh chives

1½ cups water for steaming

Chinese Steamed Egg

The smooth and silky texture of this savoury egg dish is unique. The added punch of the green onion soy drizzle will have you craving more. This is a simple version of the classic and just as delicious. You can also top it with crab or shrimp, or with mushrooms or other finely chopped vegetables. You'll need two 4-oz ramekins for this recipe.

In a small bowl, stir together the green onion, soy sauce, sambal olek, sesame oil, and fish sauce. Set aside.

Crack the eggs into a measuring cup and note the volume. Transfer to a small bowl. Measure an equal amount of water and whisk it into the eggs. Pass the mixture through a fine sieve, and then pour the egg mixture evenly into the 2 ramekins.

Pour 1½ cups of water for steaming into the pot and place the trivet in the bottom. Place the filled ramekins onto the trivet and secure the lid.

Set the machine for 2 minutes on high pressure. Allow for a 10-minute natural release before completely depressurizing the pot.

Remove the lid and carefully take out each ramekin, using canning tongs.

Drizzle the eggs with the green onion–soy mixture and serve.

Serves 2

Notes: Chopped fresh Thai red chili is a perfect substitute for sambal olek.

The proportion of egg to water is important. Some recipes call for different ratios; this one uses equal volumes of water and egg.

1 small green onion, minced

1 tbsp soy sauce

½ tbsp sambal olek (see Note)

½ tsp sesame oil

½ tsp fish sauce

2 large eggs + an equal amount water to mix with the eggs (see Note)

1½ cups water, for steaming

Strawberry Jam

This refrigerator jam is a small-batch recipe for when you want to extend the life of a few pints of fruit. No need for hours and hours of canning – just get out the electric pressure cooker and let it do the work. The recipe is for either 1 or 2 pounds of fruit. Keep the ratio at 2 parts fruit to 1 part sugar by weight and leave the other ingredients as they are. The recipe also works for raspberries and apricots.

Place the strawberries into the pot with the water and lemon juice. Secure the lid.

Set the machine for 2 minutes on high pressure. Allow for a 10-minute natural release before completely depressurizing the pot.

Remove the lid and set the machine to sauté. Add the sugar and stir well while simmering for 8–10 minutes, until the jam has reached a temperature of 215°F–220°F (102°C–104°C) or the desired thickness. (Remember, the jam will thicken slightly as it cools.)

Turn off the machine and stir in the vanilla.

Let cool slightly and transfer to sealable containers or jars and refrigerate for up to 3 months.

Makes 2 cups

Notes: If you like your jam chunky, leave the recipe as is. If you like your jam smoother but still with pieces of berry in it, use a potato masher to break down the berries after the cook. If you're the smooth type, use a hand blender to purée the jam right in the pot.

For the best jam around, make this jam at the peak of June's strawberry crop.

If you don't have a kitchen thermometer, get one. In the meantime, you can spoon a small amount of the simmering jam onto a plate to evaluate its consistency.

1 lb fresh strawberries, washed, greens removed, halved
1 tbsp water
1 tbsp lemon juice
½ lb sugar
1 tsp vanilla paste or vanilla extract

Tomato Jam

Tomato is a fruit, right? Sweet and savoury, it pairs remarkably well with cheeses such as brie, Cheddar, or blue. Tomatoes in season provide the most flavour. This recipe is perfect for those with a garden full of tomatoes ripening faster than anyone can eat them.

Place the tomatoes, shallots, ginger, salt, ground fennel seeds, ground coriander seeds, and apple cider vinegar into the pot and secure the lid.

Set the machine for 2 minutes on high pressure. Allow for a 10-minute natural release before completely depressurizing the pot.

Remove the lid and set the machine to sauté.

Add the sugar and stir well while simmering for roughly 8–10 minutes, until the jam has reached a temperature of 215°F–220°F (102°C–104°C) or the desired thickness. (Remember, the jam will thicken slightly as it cools.)

Turn off the machine and continue to stir until the simmering comes to a stop.

Let cool slightly and transfer to sealable containers or jars and refrigerate for up to 3 months.

Makes 2 cups

Note: If you don't have a kitchen thermometer, get one. In the meantime, you can spoon a small amount of the simmering jam onto a plate to evaluate its consistency.

1 lb grape or cherry tomatoes, halved
2 medium shallots, sliced
1 tbsp fresh ginger, minced
2 tsp kosher salt
1 tsp fennel seeds, ground in a mortar and pestle or spice grinder
1 tsp coriander seeds, ground in a mortar and pestle or spice grinder
¼ cup apple cider vinegar
½ lb sugar

Sour Cherry Jam

This refrigerator jam, much like the strawberry jam (page 261), is a small-batch recipe that works for either a pound or two of fruit as long as you keep the ratio at 2 parts cherries to 1 part sugar by weight. You can leave the other ingredients as they are. The recipe, with the same spices, also works for other fruit such as peaches or plums. Once cooked, you can leave the fruit whole, mash it up with a potato masher, or purée it to get the desired consistency.

Place the cardamom pods, star anise, and cinnamon stick into a spice bag.

Place the cherries into the pot with the water, lemon juice, and the spice bag. Secure the lid.

Set the machine for 2 minutes on high pressure. Allow for a 10-minute natural release before completely depressurizing the pot.

Remove the lid. Remove the spice bag and discard, and set the machine to sauté.

Add the sugar and stir well while simmering for roughly 8–10 minutes, until the jam has reached a temperature of 215°F–220°F (102°C–104°C) or the desired thickness. (Remember, the jam will thicken slightly as it cools.)

Turn off the machine and allow to cool for 5–10 minutes before transferring to sealable containers or jars.

Refrigerate for up to 3 months.

Makes 2 cups

Note: If you don't have a kitchen thermometer, get one. In the meantime, you can spoon a small amount of the simmering jam onto a plate to evaluate its consistency.

3 cardamom pods, broken
1 whole star anise
1 cinnamon stick
1 lb fresh sour cherries, washed and pitted
1 tbsp water
1 tbsp lemon juice
½ lb sugar

Blueberry Compote

This multifaceted recipe is a perfect fit for fruit-bottom cheesecake cups (page 239), among other things. Try it on pancakes, or waffles, or yogurt, or oatmeal.

Place the blueberries and 2 tbsp of water into the pot.

Set the machine for 1 minute on high pressure. Once the pressure cooking cycle has finished, depressurize completely using the quick release method.

Remove the lid and set the machine to sauté. In a small bowl, mix together the sugar, 1 tbsp of water, lemon juice, and cornstarch. Whisk this mixture into the simmering blueberries and turn off the machine.

Remove the blueberry compote from the pot and allow to fully cool before transferring to sealable containers or jars.

Refrigerate for up to 1 week.

Makes 1 cup

Notes: You can also use frozen blueberries for this recipe.

Use this recipe to make cherry compote. Substitute pitted sweet or sour cherries for the blueberries.

This recipe is easily doubled.

2 cups fresh blueberries (see Note)

2 tbsp water

2 tbsp sugar

1 tbsp water

1 tbsp lemon juice

2 tsp cornstarch

Applesauce

The best apples for this old-fashioned-tasting sauce include McIntosh, Cortland, and Gala.

Place all the ingredients into the pot and secure the lid.

Set the machine for 4 minutes on high pressure, allowing for a full natural release. If you use any form of quick release, you'll most likely see applesauce foam spurt through the release valve.

Remove the lid, remove the cinnamon stick, and whisk to break up the apples.

If you like the consistency a little looser, pack into sealable containers while the applesauce is hot. If you like it thicker, allow to fully cool, uncovered, before transferring to sealable containers.

Refrigerate for up to 2 weeks.

Makes 4 cups

3 lb apples, peeled, quartered, and cores removed
1 small stick cinnamon
½ cup water
1 tbsp lemon juice

Dulce de Leche

The Maillard reaction (page 8) at work: milk and sugar cooked together to form a rich brown caramel. Preparing this recipe is like making candy out of milk. The stovetop version requires a long, slow simmer for a few hours. This electric pressure cooker version is a far more efficient way to accomplish this sweet task. You can buy dulce de leche in stores, but it's not the same (compare the ingredient list on a can of sweetened condensed milk with that of a dulce de leche product), nor is it as satisfying as making it in your EPC.

Place the trivet in the pot and set the can in the middle of it, right-side up.

Fill the pot with water so the can is fully submerged, being careful not to overfill the pot.

Secure the lid and set the machine for 15 minutes on high pressure. Allow for a full natural release of approximately 12 hours. You're not just depressurizing the pot, but also the can within. The can will still be under pressure if its contents are hotter than room temperature. It's best to set up this recipe in the evening and do nothing else until the next morning. That way, there's no chance the can will still be hot in the pot.

Remove the lid and remove the can. You now have a can of dulce de leche to enjoy on ice cream or with fruit, or try the salted crème de dulce de leche recipe (page 243).

Once the can is open, transfer the contents to a sealable container and store, refrigerated, for up to 3 months.

Makes 1¼ cups

Caution: Do not open the can before cooking. Remove paper wrapping. Make sure can is undamaged.

Once cooked, let the can cool before handling.

1 unopened 12-oz (354 ml) can
  sweetened condensed milk,
  label removed, no dents
  (see Caution)

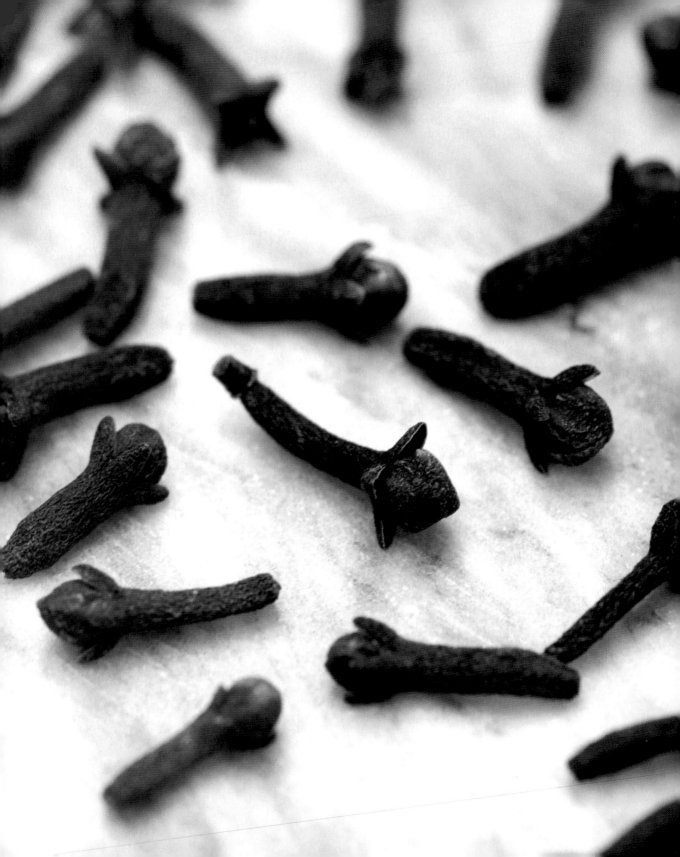

ACKNOWLEDGEMENTS

We would like to thank:

Each other for staying calm and somewhat sane and rational throughout the making of the book.

Brad Wilson at HarperCollins for trusting us with the idea, and allowing us to share our food. Writing a cookbook and making all the photographs for it is now a dream fulfilled.

Linda and Dave Wright, who went beyond normality to help us out with this project, from testing recipes to entertaining our kids for extended periods of time.

Robin Post, Peter Jarvis, Gladys Drever, Lori Shwartz, Stan Kubachek, Sue and Glen O'Brien, Kacey and Brad Clarke – our recipe testers – for all your willingness to help out. You made these recipes better.

Stephanie Boukhers, Leah Pasquale, and Brianna Kennelly, our kitchen helpers extraordinaire. Thanks for your help speeding up the process during all the photo shoots.

Patrick Engel for picking up the slack and filling in the gaps during the making of this book. For lending his expertise and producing food for the camera.

Catharine Doherty for generously supplying a selection of her wonderful props.

Tyson Lambert for lending us his EPC so we could decide whether or not we should get one. We all know how that turned out.

Inge and Wally, our neighbours and top-tier taste testers. While they always hoped for desserts, they gladly ate up the boneless rib tartine and countless others.

Ottobert Bachmaier, for Sunday afternoon chats from across the world to help us keep the vision and wiggle us free when we got stuck on something.

Lia McColl for being awesome and lending her vast knowledge of words to the project.

Lucia McColl for being analytical and honest about her likes and dislikes.

Ella McColl for being hungry.

The countless people we've shared stories, meals, recipes, and food ideas with.

Cheers and thanks to all.

INDEX